K/79

Caught by Keating

CAUGHT

Sporting Quotations from the Seventies

BY KEATING

compiled by FRANK KEATING

Cartoons by LES GIBBARD

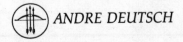 ANDRE DEUTSCH

First published 1979 by
André Deutsch Limited
105 Great Russell Street London WC1

Printed in Great Britain by
The Garden City Press Ltd
Letchworth, Hertfordshire

ISBN 0 233 97185 8

Introduction

To jog your memories I have introduced each year with a sprinkling of facts. But this little collection is by no means meant to represent a record of the 1970s, let alone a list of every gem that has been uttered. I hope only that it might be a diversion, an entertainment, a remembrance of some of the quotes and quips, writings and readings, sayings and odd snippets that have tickled my fancy through a decade of sport. I look for no more than for it to be regarded as an indipper in the Mike Procter class – quick, pithy, sometimes accurate and sometimes overpitched! If it qualifies as a bedside book, well I hope it first keeps you up late and then sends you smiling to sleep.

Frank Keating

1970

Harold Wilson called an election presuming that polling day would have England still in contention for the World Cup in Mexico. But they lost traumatically to West Germany a couple of days before the poll – and Wilson's Labour lost the election! Brazil gloriously won the Cup. It was the second of Tony Jacklin's epic golfing summers. Muhammad Ali came back triumphantly having been banned for three years after refusing to fight in Vietnam. In Britain, Henry Cooper was near the end of his long tenure as our favourite boxer. Another veteran, Brian Close, was sacked as Yorkshire's captain of cricket.

I think soccer has poetry, but I am not an authority on it. I prefer rugby and enjoy its violence – except when they start biting off ears. But I can't stand boxing: it's like a cockfight.
Elizabeth Taylor

We lost the World Cup – but it was still the finest England team I've played in. *Alan Ball*

ANN'S TWO BOOBS SINK BRITAIN
Daily Mirror headline

When you're knocked down with a good shot, you don't feel pain. In fact it's a very lovable feeling. Maybe it's like taking dope. It's like floating. You feel you love everybody – like a hippie, I guess. *Floyd Patterson*

I had asked the publishers to call my forthcoming biography 'T' Definitive Volume on t' Finest Bloody Fast Bowler that Ever Drew Breath'. But the stilly buggers just intend to call it 'Fred'. *F. S. Trueman*

George Best can do more things than anyone in all history: he is a magnificent distributor of the ball, he can beat a man on either side using methods that no one has ever before thought about, he can shoot, head, tackle and keep cooler than anyone at the same time. *Paddy Crerand*

MARK SCRATCHES AFTER 'MYSTERY' RASH
Times headline

Some women think that because they play a masculine game they have to look masculine. Some women associated with women's cricket are only ever seen in chunky sweaters and slacks. I get to the stage where I feel embarrassed with some of them. After all it doesn't take much of an effort to buy a pair of shoes with heels on. *Rachael Heyhoe, cricketer*

They've brought along this eight-year-old for coaching called Tracy Austin, from California. I saw her. I had to tell them 'How do you coach genius?' You mark my word.
Harry Hopman

Playing rugby at school I once fell on a loose ball and, through ignorance and fear, held on despite a fierce pummelling. After that it took me months to convince my teammates I was a coward. *Peter Cook*

I own three ball clubs, thirty-two top tennis pros, all kinds of little old oil wells – and one suit. You see, I do hate ostentation. *Lamar Hunt*

When I left Yale last year I thought I'd become a runner, not a doctor, much to the chagrin of my Puritan-ethic people: so I started training about 80 miles a week; then it went up to 100, then 150, then 200. Now I just run, day in day out, all the lovely year around. *Frank Shorter, marathon champion*

Brian Close's successor today as Yorkshire's captain is Geoffrey Boycott, who is intelligent and highly technically informed. He has not Close's drive nor flair, but he will make fewer mistakes and probably far fewer enemies. *John Arlott*

It remains to be seen whether Chelsea can make as much impact here in Sofia with their football as they have done with their fashion. They have already brightened the grey countenance of this Balkan city with a tapestry of colourful ties and skirts. *Yorkshire Evening Post*

It's been so long since I won a tournament, I don't know how I'd feel if it finally happened. I'd probably be so numb I wouldn't get any pleasure out of it. I'm more – lost. I went to the office today and did my job well, finished second in the Buick Open and won $14,300. I can't win anything but money. *Frank Beard, golfer*

Coaching women isn't much different from coaching men – just as long as you can remember they are women.
Hank Tauber, US ski coach

Now I must go and meet the gentlemen of the Press. They won't be too sad England lost – it will help them get me fired. *Sir Alf Ramsey*

Bedi should have been run out, but mid-on misfielded and he regained his crease after being strangled halfway down the wicket. *The Daily Telegraph*

I never eat fish. They're my friends. *Johnny Weismuller*

American girls have traditionally looked up to and emulated their favourite motion picture stars. The stars led lives that seemed exciting and far from humdrum, and young girls dreamed of leading similar glamorous lives. Now there is a new idol – and her name is Billie-Jean King.

Billie-Jean King

If Quarry's eye hadn't cut he would have licked Ali and Ali's first comeback fight would have been his only comeback fight. After three years' inactivity no boxer can come back. Ali is not a good boxer any more. He has lost his speed and he has lost his self-confidence. *Cus D'Amato*

The fact they accused Bobby Charlton of sheltering me while I 'stole' a bracelet proves I'm innocent. Bobby has never done a dishonest thing in his life. *Bobby Moore*

The present state of English rugby is serious, but not hopeless; the present state of Irish rugby is hopeless but not serious. *Noel Henderson*

JESUS SAVES – BUT ST JOHN NETS THE REBOUND *Kop graffiti*

Say mister, a good jockey don't need no orders from an owner before a race — and a bad jockey couldn't carry them out. *Jack Leach, former jockey*

Us Scots do not believe in our football team in spite of its failures, but because of them. Because we have never reached the top we can allow ourselves to feel we are always about to do so. *Willie Allan, Scots FA secretary*

Other riders are jealous of me, that's why they victimize me. I just let them get on with it. I know how to hurt them back. Just keep winning, that's all. They can't stand it.

Harvey Smith

Wee Jimmy Johnstone's ridiculous he's so good. On my first day as Scottish manager I had to call off the practice after half an hour – nobody could get the ball off Johnstone.
Tommy Docherty

Boxing should show much more concern about fighters who have almost to chop off a limb to make the weight. It nearly killed me ten years ago. It's going to kill someone in the next ten for sure. *Bobby Neill, manager*

I know it's only a matter of time before I out-lift Russia's Alexeyev. Last year the only difference between him and me was that I couldn't afford his drugs' bill. Now I can. By the next Olympics in Munich. I'll weigh about 340 lb to his 350. Then we'll see which are better, his steroids or mine.
Ken Patera, US super heavyweight

HEINZ BEANZ ARE HAZ BEENZ
telegram from Johnny Quirke to Tony O'Reilly, chairman of Heinz Inc., on his recall to Irish Rugby Union XV

Only suckers get hit with right hands.
Last words of Charley Goldman, former trainer to Rocky Marciano

Even including Becher's Brook, the Grand National obstacle that makes my heart beat fastest as your horse nears it is The Chair. It stands against the skyline, grim, tall and formidable, the rail before it a reminder of the vertitable moat that it guards, and the fence itself seeming as impenetrable as a prison wall. *John Hislop*

Don't watch Ali's gloves, arms or legs when he's fighting. Watch his brains. *Jose Torres*

A good golf course is one that makes us pros look human. It's good to see the gallery think sometimes, 'Hey, he's duffing it around just like I do.' On the other hand, we don't want too much of it: we don't want every spectator saying, 'Hell, I play as good as him: why should I waste time and money watching these jerks play.' *Arnold Palmer*

During the Irish Hare Coursing Festival week I got an order one morning from Room 152: cornflakes, bacon, egg and sausage. When I knocked on the door and then took the tray in, the man was on the floor and his dog was in the bed, and be damned if he didn't feed the whole of the breakfast to the animal. *Waiter at Clonmel Arms Hotel*

You can talk about the Rosebowl, you can have your World Series or Heavyweight Championship, but when a US oarsman, any oarsman, hears the crowd cheer at Henley he's heard everything. Anybody at Henley knows what he's talking about. They can tell you how to start, how to row the middle, when to spurt – and what the hell's wrong with your No 5 man. *Randy Jablonic, Wisconsin coach*

Women in sport? Who wants straight-legged, narrow-hipped, big-shouldered, powerful Sheilas, aggressive and ferocious in mind and body? *Percy Cerrutty, coach*

The popular assumption that professional boxers do not have brains comes from sportswriters, but then sportswriters' brains are in their turn damaged by the obligation to be clever each day. And the quantities of booze necessary to lubricate such racing of the mental gears ends up giving sportswriters the equivalent of a good many punches to the head. *Norman Mailer*

Coaching means organization and the more highly organized you are as a team the more flexible you can become.
Carwyn James, rugby coach

I often surprise myself. You can't plan some shots that go in, not unless you're on marijuana, and the only grass I'm partial to is Wimbledon's. *Rod Laver*

Would Virginia Wade have been better if it had mattered less, if she hadn't been such a perfectionist, if she had been less fascinated by what's difficult, if there had been fewer aching joys and dizzy raptures, if she hadn't begun with a devastating service and then had to learn almost everything else about the game. *David Gray*

With swim star children there is more scratching and clawing, more struggling for power, and more parasitism than anywhere in the world of sports. *Sherm Chavoor, US coach*

When I'm abroad with England I always write home to my wife and parents just before the game. It's a superstition. Before this World Cup's first game I wrote to my dad, 'I'm looking forward to getting started, but honestly we are all frightened to death'. *Alan Ball*

What do you think on the last tee before winning an Open championship? Does your life flash through your mind? Do you think of your parents, your wife, your schoolteacher, your first job? No, you just think of hitting your last drive straight. *Tony Jacklin*

I shall miss Brian Close sorely. So will all Yorkshire, and anyone who likes to see the game played with mind and muscle. If Geoffrey Boycott turns out to be half as good as Closey, then Yorkshire can consider themselves well blessed. *Michael Parkinson*

It's easy to beat Brazil. You just stop them getting twenty yards from your goal. *Bobby Charlton*

No one wins the Open. It wins you.
Doug Sanders, losing Open golfer

1971

At the beginning of the year the nation was still red-eyed from mourning the tragic death of young Lilian Board, the athlete. Ray Illingworth's MCC cricket team won the Ashes in Australia, and later that winter, Arsenal won the League and Cup soccer 'double'. In spite of competition from Lancashire's Gillette cricketers and the delightful Evonne Goolagong's win at Wimbledon, the star of the television summer was Lu Liang Huan, an unlikely Taiwanese golfer, whom the British public took to their hearts. Joe Bugner rang down the curtain on Cooper's career, and Joe Frazier looked as though he might have done the same on Ali's. The British Lions rugby side beat New Zealand – and Princess Anne was named Sportswoman of the Year.

Don't catch it, Lord, it's two strokes!
> *Lee Trevino, after Michael Bonallack's high drive in the*
> *Birkdale Open*

I did not really need to spend a penny. But I went down to the Lord's toilet, went through all the motions, even pulling the chain. The trick, the deception worked. When I came to the surface and looked at the game again, Asif was out and Lancashire were on their way. *Sir Neville Cardus*

The negro has a shorter Achilles tendon than the white, which makes swimming harder, but the reverse is true in running because it gives him greater leverage.
Norman Sarsfield, secretary, Amateur Swimming Association

Only a player himself knows which shots he's scared of hitting. *Jack Nicklaus*

You can feel just empty after losing. Life just seems to stop in a void until you surface and get it in perspective. It's all over so quickly.
> *Phil Keith-Roach, on losing the University Rugby Match*

I'm not a village idiot because I get hit on the chin. And I'm not a genius because I hit someone else on the chin. I'm no Cassius Clay, but I have my own little world. I'm Jack Bodell all of the time. *Jack Bodell*

Shall we put our heads down and make runs or get out quickly and make history?
> *Don Shepherd, greeting Peter Walker at the wicket with*
> *Glamorgan 11 for 8 against Leicestershire*

One of the factors that is making me prepare for a second Olympics was the death of Lilian Board. She was so young and she never had the chance of a second Games. It made me realize one is lucky to have the opportunity and one must not waste it. It is the story of the parable of the talents.
> *David Hemery*

My Grandad said the only way to forget about a woman is find another one. *Lee Trevino*

If I fight a grizzly bear in Red China I'd still draw a full house. *Muhammad Ali*

Very calm person make very good putt. Me try to be very calm. If I hear bird sing it's no good. Must think only of ball in hole. On the green, not bird and me. Only me. That makes very good putt. *Lu Liang Huan*

Ken Buchanan has been voted sportsman of the year by the Sports Writers' Association. The women's award went to horsewoman Anne Elizabeth Alice Louise Windsor.
Morning Star news item

John Player are getting cut-price exposure for a company banned by law for directly advertising its products on TV.
Ian Wooldridge

Banksie doesn't know how lucky he was! He bloody near got kissed on the lips in front of 40,000!
John Ritchie of Stoke City, after Banks had saved Hurst's penalty in the League Cup semi-final

Queen in rumpus at Palace. *Guardian sub-editor*

Clay is tender with his punches, lays them on as delicately as you put a postage stamp on an envelope, then cracks them in like a riding crop across your face, strikes a cruel jab like a baseball bat held head-on into your mouth, next waltzes you into a clinch with a tender arm around your neck, wings away out of reach on flying legs, digs a hook with the full swing of a baseball bat hard into your ribs, hard pokes of a jab into your face, a mocking soft flurry of pillows and gloves, a mean forearm cuts you off from coming on him, a cool wrestle of your neck in a clinch, then elusive again, gloves snakelip your face like a whip. *Norman Mailer*

Knott and Engineer are probably the happiest Test cricketers in the business. *Brian Scovell*

Now we're going places.
> *Andy Smith, after Bugner had beaten Cooper*

I watch all his fights and get so proud when he sweeps up in his silver gown. *Mrs Jackie 'TV' Pallo*

Sure he was awkward, he felt awkwardly.
> *Jerry Quarry, after beating Bodell in sixty-four seconds*

When I got to the final, I asked someone to pinch me to make sure it was really happening.
> *Evonne Goolagong at Wimbledon*

Sorry. *John Snow*

If the ILTF and the WCT were the Russians and Americans we'd all be dead by now. *John Newcombe*

It would be wrong for me to disclose how much showjumpers earn since it could bring about Inland Revenue problems.
> *Jack Webber, British Show Jumping secretary*

I resent you calling the matchmaker, Mr Michael Duff, 'my henchman', he is in fact my 'right-hand man'.
> *Mike Barrett, boxing promoter*

I recently bought three books by Russia's Nobel prizewinner, Alexander Solzhenitsyn. *George Best*

Get the gun ready, we're going to set traps.
 Muhammad Ali, immediately after defeat by Frazier

When I retired I was twenty-two. A swimmer does not get punched or clobbered, no cuts, bruises or broken bones, and I was an amateur not a professional; but I had had it. I was tired and I had been tired for three years.
 Don Schollander, US champion swimmer

It takes more than a war to stop the Indians enjoying their hockey. *Pat Rowley*

I am at last beginning to know what dear old Gilbert Harding meant when he described himself as a 'telephoney'.
 Henry Longhurst

Frazier is not a ugly as Liston, but there's not much in it.
 Muhammad Ali

Rugby is not all that important to me. I just play for the fun of it. It's not the most vital thing in life is it? *Barry John*

There is a narcissism in every referee. I honestly believe that a great many referees around the world have effeminate tendencies.
 Joao Saldhana, former Brazilian soccer manager

For the Davis Cup you have to have separate bedrooms from your husband while he is in training. You spend the whole of the year living with him then all of a sudden they say, 'No, no, naughty, not the night before the Davis Cup.' I suppose it's because they are representing England. *Mrs Mark Cox*

What is it, being a footballer? If you take away Match of the Day and the Press and the fans and hangers-on, it's all very empty and lonely. *Rodney Marsh*

Try explaining cricket to an intelligent foreigner; it is far harder than explaining Chomsky's generational grammar.
C. P. Snow

The competitor in lane four is a real competitor.
David Coleman

Because football is so badly reported a great number of spectators are ignorant about the game. One solution might be to cut down on the free drink provided in the Press box.
Patrick Marnham, Telegraph magazine

We're treated like schoolchildren by the Board. Run here, don't run there, is all we get. We're amateur sportsmen. Why can't we decide our own lives? *Dick Taylor*

Sir Learie Constantine belongs to that rare and tiny group of athletes whose deeds are not printed in record books but burned on the mind. We shall miss him, except when we remember him, when he was in his prime and beautiful.

Michael Parkinson

The Greek squad to face Neasden in the second leg of the Inter-Suburbs European Nations Cup was named in Athens yesterday. It reads: Xenophon, Egganchippolatas, Aristophones, Menopaus, Owa'alotigotides, Kikiminthebolox, Logarithm, Thycydides, Chrystalpallas, Delicatessen, Underneathearchas. *Lord Gnome*

I am still badly feeling the effect of my injury and will not be returning to the Yorkshire side for some time.

Geoff Boycott, after scoring 138 not out in a club match for Leeds

Trousers are now allowed to be worn by ladies on the course. But they must be removed before entering the clubhouse.

Notice in Irish golf club

If I can see 'em I can hit 'em.

Lancashire's David Hughes at 9 pm before scoring 24 in an over to win Gillette Cup semi-final

We were all running for Lilian.

Vera Nicholl, 800 metres winner in Helsinki

I am still looking for shoes that will make running on streets seem like running barefoot across the bosoms of maidens.

Dave Bronson, US marathon runner

I find I am playing every ball, bowling every ball and fielding every ball. The captaincy has cost me over six hundred runs a season. I am snapping at my wife and children and sleeping no more than four hours a night.

Mickey Stewart, captain of Surrey, the County Champions

Well, Jack, at least you won the first round.

Reporter to Bodell after he lost to Urtain in two rounds

Every team has a clogger whose job is to put a clever opponent out of the match. *Harry Catterick, manager of Everton*

I wouldn't want to be a referee under the present system because I'd need the IQ of a super university professor.

Alan Hardaker, soccer official

After fifty metres out from the finish I began to think I've won, that's it. I had a feeling of contentment, almost complacency. And that's when, unforgivably, I lost my concentration. They all came up on me and with a shock I thought, blast, I've lost. Then I thought, never mind, I'm only nineteen.
David Jenkins, after winning the European 400 metres in Helsinki

Sunday Game: USA v Rest of the World. Loser Buys Beer.
Extract from newsletter of Manhattan RFC, New York

The ref could not speak a word of English, but he spoke German all right. Overath spent the whole match chatting him up. *Frank McLintock*

Come on. No, wait. Get back . . . sorry. *Geoff Boycott*

The referee counted too fast.
Chuck Olivares explaining his knockout by Danny McAlinden

Of course a player can have sexual intercourse before a match and play a blinder. But if he did it for six months he'd be a decrepit old man. It takes away the strength from the body.
Bill Shankly, manager of Liverpool

I know a bit more about form than I did in my army days.
Lord Wigg

To walk from the squash court to the dressing room as weak as a kitten, sweat dripping off you but mind as clear as tomorrow's dawn, is better than five reefers or a trip on LSD. *John Hopkins*

The crowds tell me to go home or catch a banana boat. I just laugh. With Charlie George it's his long hair. With me it's my colour. *Brendon Batson, Grenada-born Arsenal reserve*

There are, they say, fools, bloody fools, and men who remount in a steeplechase. *John Oaksey*

After sweatin' in fields all day as I did, I'm not goin' to stand for all that Uncle Tom crap. *Joe Frazier*

English is difficult. I speak only Hong Kong golf English. When I go professional I take teacher, say must speak English. Every day it is A–B–C–D, A–B–C–D. But no A–B–C–D in golf, only 1–2–3–4, maybe 5. So I take another teacher. *Lu Liang Huan*

1972

The reek of smoke following the murders at the Munich Olympics hung like a pall over the whole year. To record the names of such as Spitz, Korbut and Peters still seems slightly irrelevant. George Best's longtime disenchantment with Manchester United (and vice versa) was emerging at the same time as the nation's growing enchantment with Brian Clough and his vibrant new side at Derby. At cricket, England retained the Ashes in a dull summer, Lester Piggott won his sixth Derby on Roberto, and Stan Smith beat the mercurial Ilie Nastase in an epic Wimbledon final.

When I first got back to Belfast with my gold medal the soldiers had a geiger counter which went click, click, click. 'You've got a large piece of metal in there,' they said. But I ended up signing their flak jackets. *Mary Peters*

Rugby football is, first and foremost, about attitudes. Unless the approach is right the basics and the skills will suffer and no values of any dimension, least of all aesthetic, will be achieved. *Carwyn James*

As much as I want to win as many tournaments as I can, I am not prepared to play, week in week out, year after year, as Gary Player does. *Tony Jacklin*

I have been banned from umpiring at Wimbledon for not wearing a tie. I've not, in fact, been wearing one there for eight years. I doubt if I'll be back.
Gerald Garside, tennis umpire

What they say about footballers being ignorant is rubbish. I spoke to a couple yesterday and they are quite intelligent.
Raquel Welch

I've never been a good professional cricketer . . . I'm bloody marvellous for three days on the trot, very good for another day, but, in terms of concentration, not so hot for the next two or three. *Tony Lewis*

I did not enjoy 'The Godfather' at all. *Bobby Moore*

I'm not a naturally modest bloke. *Charlie George*

Marsh might hit sixes, but he is not a slogger. I would call him a Very Scientific Hard Hitter. *Jack Fingleton*

We were going to Portugal for our holiday, but now it looks like Bermuda – that may be just far enough away to steer clear of George Best and all his problems. *Bobby Charlton*

No one could be utterly dull in the presence of Katharine, Duchess of Kent. *E. W. Swanton*

Speed? Really the whole process is the reverse of speed, how to eliminate it. It doesn't exist for me except when I am driving poorly. Then things seem to be coming at me quickly instead of passing in slow motion and I know I'm off form.
Jackie Stewart

I am glad I have not got a big serve – because I fear for the size of my shoulders. *Françoise Durr*

Weightlifting is a sport that gets lost in the suburbs. It is private, obsessive. I'm not at all interested in sport – I am interested in obsessions. *Mai Zetterling in Munich*

There is blood on my typewriter, blood on my notes, blood on my programme. And however long I live I will never forget the face of Ron Stander standing up to Joe Frazier. The face of courage in tears. *Peter Wilson*

We must get away from the idea that sport is the prerogative of youth. *Eldon Griffiths, Minister of Sport*

If another jockey asks you for a bit of room at a fence, you bloody well give it. Next time you might be asking him. There's quite enough trouble out there without making any of our own. *Terry Biddlecombe*

Ex-Manchester United players are meant to have wings on their feet or something. *Francis Burns*

If I died tomorrow, I'd be quite happy. Even being barracked at Fulham was a pleasure, though I didn't think so at the time. *Jimmy Hill*

A distinguished professor of pathology, who recently holed out in one at the fourth at Walton Heath, thus opening the round with 4371444, asks whether he is the only man in history to have started a round of golf with his own telephone number. *Henry Longhurst*

I am the first Asian to play multi-racial sport in South Africa. True, they didn't expect me to turn up, but if they've accepted one they will accept millions.
Sharif Khan, Pakistani squash player

If someone says I'm not feminine, I say 'screw it'.
Rosie Casals

When a horse hits a fence his speed decelerates in a split second while the jockey's body goes straight on. Overcoming this distressing tendency is one of the skills a rider had better acquire if he wants to stay in the business. *Lord Oaksey*

Dark clouds are coming up from the south-west – and I'm sorry to tell you that the wind is blowing in the same direction. *Brian Johnston*

I like Jacky Ickx, but his temperament is uneven. You see it in his driving. He will do a few good corners, then a bad one; a few fast laps, then a slow one. There is no continuity. He thinks we are all test pilots. *Jackie Stewart*

At the end of my life I could well look back and think that Munich was my finest hour. In sport you either get tremendous fulfilment or tremendous disappointment. Nothing else in life is ever so cut and dried. *Richard Meade*

I am the greatest single skuller in Argentina. I am the only single skuller in Argentina. *Alberto Demiddi*

Mark Cox is suddenly like the rugby player who has learned to tackle low. He's not afraid to skin his knee these days.
John Newcombe

Liverpool are the most uncomplicated side in the League – they drive forward when they've got the ball and get behind it when they haven't. *Joe Mercer*

My mother was up there in the stand. She doesn't know a bugger about rugby, but she knows we won.
Delme Thomas, Llanelli's captain

I never liked sailing men. They yell blue murder at you all day, but then, when the boat is moored, the whisky comes out. Captain Bligh turns Casanova and is all ready to seek out your jolly erogenous zones and play deck coitus. *Jilly Cooper*

In Seville, peeping through an iron grilled casement, but inside no Barber, only two nuns glued to a quacking television set showing 'Match of the Day'.
Philip Hope-Wallace

I make a habit of never butting anyone because I cut so easily. *Wyn Davies*

If my mother hadn't thrown my football boots on the fire I might have become as famous as Denis Compton. *Len Hutton*

Good-looking American gentleman of fifty would like to share tickets for Olympics with nice Bavarian lady, view to also enjoying what translates decorously as happy togetherness. *Ad in German press*

A lot of boxing promoters couldn't match the cheeks of their own backside. *Mickey Duff, matchmaker*

The men who run racing reflect the picture of the country as I see it – a group of political, social and economical mules. I wouldn't normally expect to mix with them, nor they me.
Lord Wigg

I can find no factual evidence that sexual activity in moderation up to and including the night before a match has any detrimental effect. About half an hour of sexual activity, if appropriate, maximizes the onset, quantity and quality of sleep.
Dr Craig Sharp, consultant to British Olympic canoe squad

Billie-Jean King's father put her into tennis to stop her being a woman wrestler. *Jim Murray, Los Angeles Times*

Frazier is so ugly that he should donate his face to the US Bureau of Wild Life. *Muhammad Ali*

If they knee me I butt 'em. *Charlie George*

Good athletes laugh easily, dull ones are hard to work with.
Alec Stock, Fulham's manager

I am determined that my twin sons shall not take up throwing events; unless you take steroids you have no chance.
Howard Payne

My grandfather couldn't prescribe a pill to make a greyhound run faster, but he could produce one to make the other five go slower. *Benny Green*

Recently my coach underwent a course on Attacking Football run by the FA. He did not see a goal scored on the whole course. *Alec Stock*

Racing is like politics – it's full of good rogues. *Eddie Harty*

When cricketers scowl and chew gum the result is highly unattractive. But Barry Richards completes a perfect technical picture of bland assurance unmarred by a rotating jaw.
E. W. Swanton

Harry, you're not as dumb as you look.
Muhammad Ali to Harry Carpenter

How can we be called racialist when there are no non-whites who can play or watch squash in South Africa.
Bill Emmett, Chairman South Africa SRA

We despise them, we despise them. *Cambridge's*
huddled halftime chant during Varsity rugby match

I will not have cloggers in my side at Derby. I would not have fielded the teams Sir Alf Ramsey did against West Germany or Scotland. They were violent, brutal games.
Brian Clough

My Keith is a quiet boy about the house and he never minds lending a hand with the washing up. *Keith Murdoch's mum*

Sheila Sherwood told me that I blew so many kisses to the crowd after every jump that I could have got the job at the very end of the Morecambe and Wise Show. *Mary Peters*

The real loser of our times is the one who is expected to win. That is why I was so interested in making a film of David Bedford. *Claude Lelouch*

Racing must be run by professionals. It's just not good enough for a man to join the Salvation Army for a few weeks, become a Brigadier, and then walk into a top job at the Jockey Club. *John Banks, bookmaker*

Outside a car the late Jim Clark was one of the most disorganized men I've known. He couldn't make up his mind. He hadn't a full fingernail; he ate them; he bit back to the skin on his first joint. But he drove with a certainty that was near flawless. *Jackie Stewart*

People go to Laver to talk about tennis – they come to me to talk about abortions. *Billie-Jean King*

Pele couldn't get into my squad the way my lads are playing these days. *Pat Saward, Brighton manager*

Oh dear, he's laddered his tights.
Kent Walton, wrestling commentator

This Australian side do not agree that Boycott is the best bat in the world; to them the accolade is firmly held by Barry Richards, followed by their own Gregg Chappell.
Jack Fingleton

If you don't do something special against Chris Evert you find yourself losing concentration after thirty-five shots.
Julie Heldman

There never was a good skipper of a bad side. And I've got a great one. I could go out with any one of them tonight just as easily as I could with my wife.
Lancashire's captain Jack Bond

There is someone, somewhere, who could do for Virginia Wade what Franz Stampfl did for Roger Bannister.
Chris Brasher

Ah, cricket, the sight of bowler and players genuinely applauding a century against them. If a Rangers soccer side stood to applaud a Celtic goal I'd know the age of miracles had come. Cricket's greatness lies in the ability of players to honour a foe. It's the way life should be lived.
Professor William Barclay

No team has worked harder than the winners of that match – or indeed the losers.
Barry Davies, BBC commentator

Few people who watch soccer know what goes on between two men marking each other. It's personal, private, putting your soul on the line. *Charlie Cooke*

I must have kept wicket, day in day out, to Derek Underwood for seven years now and I doubt if he's bowled ten full-tosses or long-hops in the whole of that time. *Alan Knott*

And there's Brinkley at the back – quite content to let Spitz set the pace. *BBC swimming commentator*

I know it's said I can't punch but you should see me putting the cat out of a night. *Chris Finnegan*

CBK—3**

No, I have never been to a psychiatrist. I hate being analysed by friends because they never put you back together again.
Virginia Wade

I could have kept my title by leaving Iceland when Fischer first failed to arrive, but I thought, when I come to the end of my life, when I'm about to die, I'll say, 'What a fool to miss the most interesting match of my life because of some quarrel over formalities.' *Boris Spassky*

The only thing to change the South African Government's sports policy would be when the Springbok rugby team was ostracized internationally. *Mike Procter*

If you put monkeys on to play they'd still pack the Centre Court at Wimbledon. *Neale Fraser*

Rodney has more skill than anyone in English football. He affects people – like Bestie, Cassius Clay or Tom Jones. I don't know what it is but he's got it. *Malcolm Allison*

Brigadier Gerard did not win the Derby because he did not run in it. He did not run in it because he was not bred for it. He wasn't bred for it because I couldn't afford it.
John Hislop, owner

I've never taken anything on tour but grey slacks and the All Black blazer. It's all you've got to wear, it's all you want to wear. *Ian Kirkpatrick*

Who wants to win something runs a hundred metres; who wants to experience something runs a marathon.
Emil Zatopek

My Dad's greatest claim to fame is that he went to school with John Arlott. *Graham Roope*

Margaret Court plays in such run-of-the-mill garments. I reproach her for it and decry her influence on the game and attitude to the public. The stars who don't care a damn how they look are amateurs. *Teddy Tinling*

Mark Spitz talks a lot about himself. But how can you blame him? That's the only thing people ask him about.
Dave Edgar, US swimmer

We do not run for any flag or organization, we run for ourselves. *Vince Matthews, US runner*

The only time our girls looked good at Munich was in the Village discotheque between nine and eleven every night.
US coach

The Ancient Greeks kept women athletes out of their Games. They wouldn't even let them on the sidelines. I'm not so sure but that they were right. *Avery Brundage*

The only man who can beat Bedford is Bedford himself.
Ron Clarke, runner

I'd rather win six out of six, or even four out of four, than six out of seven. My self-esteem comes into it. I just don't want to lose. *Mark Spitz, swimmer*

I'm afraid that today I only had to give ninety per cent of what I really have. *Valery Borzov, 100 metres gold medallist*

I've led a calm life and can't think that those sportsmen in that building are going to get killed. They should shut this whole place down. Running is not all that important.
Hailu Ebba, Ethiopian runner

We took turns on the terrace, plucking seeds from a fennel plant and grinding them in our palms. Below, people played chess or ping-pong. The trading of Olympic pins continued. Athletes sunbathed by the pool. It seemed inappropriate, but what was one supposed to do?

Kenny Moore, US distance runner

I still believe in the Olympic idea. Communication between countries is essential; the Games should be a time when the world can step back – two weeks when the people can watch the young and enthuse about health and happiness and joy and peaceful struggles. *David Hemery*

1973

Two legendary performances: Sunderland won the Cup – and never did anything again; Red Rum won the first of his three Grand Nationals – and never looked back. England lost to Poland and failed to qualify for the World Cup and the guillotine was prepared for Sir Alf Ramsey. But Liverpool, under Shankly, began their relentless march through the rest of the decade. Jan Kodes won a debased Wimbledon at which many of the leading players refused to play. Joe Frazier was thrashed by George Foreman and Ken Norton broke Ali's jaw. There was another sad death in motor sport when François Cevert was killed – but, thankfully, Jackie Stewart decided to retire.

Pity I didn't get me eyebrows on telly sooner; really you can cop a lot of easy loot in this panel game lark, can't you?
Terry Venables, footballer

I was able to stay in my natural environment and develop there and become a respected member of the community. But if I was taken as a fifteen-year-old from Belfast and pitched into Old Trafford I really feel I would have reacted just as George Best has. I could not have stood it.
Barry John

Maybe I am not the greatest British heavyweight champion that ever lived. *Danny McAlinden*

The World Cup without England will be like a wedding without the bride, a party without champagne.
Editorial in Cologne newspaper

Some people think football is a matter of life and death. I don't like that attitude. I can assure them it is much more serious than that. *Bill Shankly*

If West Ham's soccer is unhealthy, then English soccer's unhealthy. *Joe Mercer*

When anybody starts calling me a Messiah, all I have to do is go and see my parents. *Bob Stokoe*

The money I've made has no correlation with the validity of my statements. *Mark Spitz, millionaire*

People see my swing and say: 'Oh what a beautiful swing', and I always want to reply: 'Yeah but why doesn't it work better?' *Tommy Aaron*

English football has degenerated to unbelievable levels. The hackers are now completely in charge. *Johnny Byrne*

My back is ruined so I can't sit still for long. The game has given me arthritis in my neck from butting people with my head, and if I walk too much my knees swell.
Peter Gent, 31, retiring US footballer

I am not unhappy to be hit for six sixes. I want batsmen to play shots. Only then I can get them out! *Bishen Bedi*

There's a lot more to getting to the top at judo than running round Regent's Park in thumping great boots.
Dave Starbrook

On the golf course, unlike films, when you are good and ready, you hit it. And when you have made a mess of it, there is absolutely nobody to blame but yourself, your own greed and your own stupidity. To me it has a pure practical, quasi-religious quality about it. Ultimate total responsibility. *Guy Hamilton, film director*

The Queen Mother always rings me after any of her horses has run and says: 'How are my darlings?'
Jack O'Donoghue, trainer

I want to prove that women are lousy. They stink. They don't belong on the same court as a man. *Bobby Riggs*

If it is possible to make a million out of soccer, I would like to be the first to do it. *Bobby Moore*

Football is business, and business is business.
Rinus Michels, Barcelona coach

I have always felt I would retire when I stopped enjoying racing, but it occurred to me recently that I may have to find another reason because I may never stop enjoying it.

Graham Hill

Jack Solomons was a legend who has now become a myth. He is still a considerable nuisance value, a destructive element, that's all. *Jarvis Astaire*

I can't tell you what I really think about Jarvis Astaire because I know the laws of libel too well. *Jack Solomons*

I asked the All England Club for two tickets for friends to watch me in the quarter-finals. I did not mind being refused as much as the manner. It was dreadful – as if I were asking for £100,000. If it had happened a week before I would have walked out with all the others. *Jan Kodes*

Someone said that no one 'murders' Troon. The way I played the Open they couldn't even arrest me for second degree manslaughter. *Lee Trevino*

Every sportsman is an egoist. *Jim Fox*

I owe it all to my wife. She does not like me to be angry on court. So when the ball goes three yards out and the line-judge is asleep, I no longer tell him what I think. I say to myself 'Be calm', and now I am the big sport, yes?

Ilie Nastase

I don't drop players, I make changes. *Bill Shankly*

Jackie Stewart faces two options, neither of them very appealing. He can quit racing and save his life, or he can quit racing and lose what his life is about.

François Çevert, the day before he died

I have to play bloody well for months in the US to earn $100,000 and then half of that goes to taxes and expenses. I can make more in Europe and go to more exciting places. In the US every tournament seems like the same place.

Tony Jacklin

Few teams in the history of football can have leapt to fame as rapidly as Sunderland. The Club was founded in 1879.
FA Year Book 1973-74

The irony is that if Sir Alf felt obliged to quit he might well be leaving the best side he has ever had. *Jimmy Hill*

I retired because I was sick at the lack of control exercised by the Boxing Board. Years ago I warned the secretary that one day one lot was going to walk into his office and send him out for a pot of tea and he would have to go and get it. *Jim Wicks*

I don't stand there and look at the ball and wiggle the club like Arnold Palmer and them cats. I walk up and hit it about 350 yards. I figure I could drive longer if I ran up and hit it.
Muhammad Ali

Dave Bedford amazes me: the gay bachelor with his car and his new job. The way he packs it all in: he'll run 14 miles at 7 am and another 14 at 5 pm and then go out to eat and drink. I just couldn't do it. He can. *Brendan Foster*

I don't have any money. I'm about broke. I can't get any of the money I've won. I'm supposed to have a lot of contenders knocking at my door, but when I open it they aren't there.
George Foreman

Short odds and betting tax have put the professional punter out of business. The rest of the betting public only accept the odds because they don't realize what's happening. Odds are so short today that you just can't get on some horses.

Richard Baerlein

Winning is a drug. Once you have experienced it, you cannot do without it. You live for it. *Bernard Hunt*

Whaddya mean giving one of my players orange juice? I'm not having him spoiling his beauty sleep by having to get up in the night for a pee. *Bill Shankly*

I want to rest my bones, rest my body and go lay on some beach and forget this mess. I'll have a $20,000 cheque coming to me every month. Beautiful. *Muhammad Ali*

The great failing of modern football is the amount of inter-passing without gain. *Walter Winterbottom*

I know exactly how George Best feels. If I were him I'd be running away every week. *David Bedford*

I'll never be accepted by some of the snob Press.

Ray Illingworth

Apart from Neale and Taylor, I can still lick the rest of the England players without any practice – that's how bad the standard is in this country. *Chester Barnes*

I don't care about politics. The impact of soccer is much healthier and deeper than politics. *Johann Cruyff*

Very modest people often have a great deal to be modest about. *Jarvis Astaire*

As for the accidents and tragedy – the circus goes on. There's no room for tears.

François Çevert, the day before he died

The day I pack it in I'll heave an almighty sense of relief.

Steve Heighway

There's no fun in soccer any more. It's all deadly serious. We'll end up playing in cemeteries. *Terry Venables*

I'm very placid most of the time, but I blow up very quickly. I shout and I wave my arms, my lip twitches. I become incoherent, and I swear. All at the same time. *Jack Charlton*

Any British side that tries to beat Lazio at their own game soon discover that the Italians have a big advantage in terms of match practice. *Hugh McIlvanney*

Now I look at it all out there on the field and think, crikey, was I ever in the middle of that lot? *Barry John*

Matches are won and lost between Monday and Friday – not on Saturday afternoons. *Peter Taylor, football manager*

Any British boxer fighting in Italy has to knock his man out to be even worth a draw. *Bunny Sterling*

Strikers today don't seem to need any stitches. Forty times my face was cut so badly it needed stitching. And they say it's harder now. *John Charles*

St Anthony, Blessed Oliver Plunkett and St Theresa: many thanks for finding lost UEFA Cup ticket.

Ad in Liverpool Echo

Footballers' wives should be seen and not heard.

Tony Walters

I may not make myself popular saying it, but the decline of cricket as a character builder has had a lot to do with our present situation. As soon as soccer became the so-called national sport, the whole idea of a game that was played for its own sake among people who understood each other went by the board. *Frederick Raphael*

In all the years that I have known the Queen Mother she has never asked me or any of her friends to place a bet for her on one of her horses. *Sir Martin Gilliat, Private Secretary*

Hello and welcome to this great week of show-jumping, and as I say in this week of show-jumping we won't just be seeing show-jumping we'll be seeing all the people who make show-jumping such a spectacle this week, this week of show-jumping in which, as I say, 49 qualifiers for tonight's event have been simmered down to those 21 people who'll make this night of show-jumping not just part of this great week we've been looking forward to as I say, but the people who, the people who . . .
David Vine, BBC commentator

Should anything go wrong with me now, mentally or physically, I can only blame God. I can only blame something that I can't control. *Joe Bugner*

After a match, whether I win or lose, I never fail to thank God. I need God's help. And if I play with that need I feel at peace. Of course, I must also try. If I close my eyes and say 'God help me' and do nothing myself, that is foolishness.
Muhammad Lafir, world billiards champion

Those who tell you it's tough at the top have never been at the bottom. *Joe Harvey*

The threat to Wimbledon and Europe is what is going to happen in the States, not poor Nikki Pilic. *Donald Dell*

Mark Cox, the tennis player, pays his gardener more than our top table-tennis players can earn in a week.
Chester Barnes

Arnold Palmer used to throw a club now and then. So did I. But now I never blame the course or the caddies or the galleries. When I play rotten golf now I only blame myself. You see I'm a perfectionist. *Tom Weiskopf*

In the old days at competitions, people would cluster round the champions asking them about their exercise routines. Now they just ask 'What drugs are you on?'
Bodybuilder Roger Walker, third in Mr Britain

Football has become a vast bore. Sports editors and producers who have so often allowed key space to be occupied by football trivia, because of cricket's weakness back in the sixties, may soon have to think again. Cricket has for the moment the priceless gift of variety. *Robin Marlar*

Winning is easy. It's far harder, once you've won, to lose honourably. I suppose I'll be beaten eventually. I only hope I accept it graciously. *Rodney Pattison*

You cameramen are getting my goat. Horses are very sensitive. They are not like humans. They don't understand what all the fuss is about. *Princess Anne*

When they told me Foreman had beaten Frazier, I thought: My, my, there goes five million dollars. *Muhammad Ali*

Crystal Palace's psychiatrist tells us that people who are friends pass more to each other. *Malcolm Allison*

Today's Radio: 11 am Test Match Special. Hans Keller discusses the influence of Schoenberg on the bowling of Chandrasekhar Ravi-Shankar (4 – 31). *Lord Gnome*

Rugby people, who I knew to be kind, thoughtful socialists still wrap the cloak of the game around themselves when it comes to touring South Africa. *John Morgan*

Up in the press box at the Grand National are all the racing journalists, backs to the field, straining to get a peek at the TV set to see what's happening. *Stanley Reynolds*

It's tight, taut and muscular. Bobby Moore's posterior comes top of our Girls' Bottom League. *The Sun*

Some years ago I sparred with Frazier. He whacked me four times in the cobblers and didn't say sorry once; he was champion so I had to grin and bear it. *Joe Bugner*

So over to the ringside – Harry Commentator is your carpenter. *BBC announcer*

The severest criticism of Ray Illingworth is that he did not sufficiently discourage the element of selfishness which is part of most successful cricketers. *Mike Brearley*

E. W. Swanton – Sort of a Cricket Peron.
Headline in Jamaican Daily Gleaner

We're really going all out not to finish last.
George Newton, British weightlifter at world championships

A pub called the 'Sir Alf Ramsey' will attract all the wrong sort of person. *Tunbridge Wells resident*

Jockeys are only really there to win on the ones that aren't meant to win. *Terry Biddlecombe*

Of course we are going to continue playing in Europe. How else can we all get duty free cigarettes.
John Cobbold, Ipswich Town chairman

I'm the last of the amateurs – and considering how I jump I reckon it's just as well.
Mike Campbell, British high-jump champion

Which side went out to retaliate first? *Danny Blanchflower*

Why didn't they tell us that England's centre-forward was, in fact, a Polish agent called Shivas. *Clive James*

With Jimmy Hill a little humility would work wonders.
Brian Glanville

Soccer is run by second-rate con-men. Petit-bourgeois, frustrated small businessmen. It's a tragedy because, socially, football is very important. *Eamon Dunphy*

What's wrong with the game? Too many David Colemans, who know it all, for a start. And too many pooftas, flash types: 'It's the in thing, duckey'. They don't know Alan Ball from Charlie George yet they prance around here after leaving their flash cars, Jensens and that, over in Finsbury Park or Green Lanes, so they won't get damaged by us nasty lads. Well, one of these days, they're in for a shock.
Frank Rowe, 17, Arsenal supporter

1974

Alf Ramsey took his leave and after a breezy interim under Joe Mercer, Don Revie took over the England side and was on the sidelines for both Leeds' losing European Cup final and the World Cup, which was won by the hosts, West Germany. The Scots played fitfully, and though they did not lose a game they failed to qualify for the closing stages. At rugby, England beat Wales for what turned out to be the only time in the decade, and the British Lions easily beat South Africa. Jimmy Connors and Chris Evert announced themselves (and for a time, their love) by winning the respective singles titles at Wimbledon. Ali regained his title against Foreman in an astonishing 'rumble in the jungle'.

CBK—4**

How much? *Franz Beckenbauer*

To fight in South Africa would be an affront to my family, my country and my integrity. *John Conteh*

If I get a £5 speeding fine it's all over the front pages. If I win the Grand Prix of Rotterdam, one of the greatest of all titles, the back pages don't even mention it. *Harvey Smith*

The quiet of the church was shattered by rhythmic clapping and the shouting of 'England' as Rev. Stevens spoke of the patriotism of St George being manifested in the cry for England's football team. *Twickenham Times*

It was always football for me: when girls at school passed me love letters under the desk, I flicked them back. I never squeezed the spots on my face 'cos I wanted to be repulsive and keep the girls away. *Alan Ball*

I don't know why prop-forwards bother to play rugby.
Lionel Weston, scrum-half

If the British working man backs a horse or a dog because of its breeding, why should not the better-bred members of the House of Lords be worthy of our trust in their inherited powers of leadership. *Letter in The Daily Telegraph*

I turned to God at sea: I prayed every day. Never on land. You know how insignificant you are at sea; on land it seems to matter that you change your car each year. *Chay Blyth*

If you lose a race it's a matter of passing the buck: the owner blames the trainer, the trainer blames the jockey, the jockey blames the poor old horse. *Tony Murray*

Football is about playing: if you don't turn up at 3 pm that's it. A lot of bullshit is being talked about football and pop: Dylan doesn't have to give concerts week in week out. Footballers can't record their skills on plastic. Elvis didn't have to come to England to be Elvis – but Best had to go to Old Trafford to be Best. *Steve Grant*

Profit isn't a dirty word nowadays. Money is how we keep the score in motor racing nowadays. *Colin Chapman*

A chronic gambler who says he backed a winning horse every time he prayed in church for help to clear his debts was so impressed by the power of prayer that he has become a Catholic priest. *The Daily Telegraph*

I was a pretty sport until at parties I learned that when you were playing piano there was always a pretty girl standing at the bassclef end of the instrument. I ain't been no athlete since. *Duke Ellington*

Deaf viewers are to protest about the language by players on 'Match of the Day'. Although most viewers could not distinguish the words, the country's deaf lip-read the exchange.
The Daily Telegraph

Bring back Ward! *Sun, northern edition, August 16*

Bring back Snow! *Sun, southern edition, August 16*

No European gentleman would act like Mr Havelange has.
Sir Stanley Rous

Footballers now know money business better than football business. *Joao Saldanha*

Graduate required for coaching to Greek at O-level. N. London area. References essential. Pupil unenthusiastic. Good rowing man would be ideal. *Ad in Private Eye*

I enjoy hitting a batsman more than getting him out. I like to see blood on the pitch. And I've been training on whisky.
Jeff Thomson

I had never admired a man as much as Matt Busby. But when I left Old Trafford I had never been let down by any man as much as by him. *Frank O'Farrell*

Tournament director Tony Pickard took an extremely strong line on Nastase's withdrawal and said today: 'If he doesn't come – he doesn't'. *Notts Evening Post*

It was the sort of football that would bring the crowds in any Saturday of the week. *Walley Barnes on West Ham v. Wolves*

STOP PRESS: Modern Decameron (Women's Heats): I, J. Tweedie (US); 2, M. Kenny (Eire); 3, Sun Tan (Formosa). British Placing: 750th F. N. Starborgling (no relation). Also ran and ran: F. Cashin (D. Sketch). *Lord Gnome*

ATP, WTT, WCT, ILTF – there's everything but the B and O Railroad. It's now as absurd as an Abbott and Costello comedy routine – and look what happened to vaudeville.
Fred Perry

The only word never used to describe what happens in football is 'kick'. The ball is always 'volleyed' or 'struck' or 'driven'. 'Kick' only happens when players do it to each other. *Penelope Gilliat*

Ten times or so in my career I have experienced a state where everything is pure, vividly clear. I'm in a cocoon of concentration, and I'm invincible. *Tony Jacklin*

Don't bother with Ascot unless you remember to raise your topper to the Queen's representative, the Marquis of Abergavenny (pronounce it Ab-venny), and to totally remove your hat if a member of the Royal Family happens to pass by. But don't cheer please. *Paul Callan*

I am expecting a call from Tottenham – and there again I am not expecting one, if you see what I mean.
Danny Blanchflower

The Lynn and West Norfolk FA Commission are still making enquiries about the abandoned Upwell Res v. Southery match, because the game was resumed with a completely different referee and with the same player who had been sent off by the first referee. *East Anglian Times*

A high degree of skill and intelligence are required for croquet and therefore it is not going to attract the lower income groups. *Croquet Association chairman, quoted in The Times*

Welsh supporters are one-eyed and Welsh players are cheats.
Sid Going, New Zealand rugby player

The Australian Government should deport the English geriatrics now posing as cricketers. And the MCC should be charged with fraud under the Trade Practices Act.
Barry Cohen, Labour MP

Girls who ride horses don't necessarily have big behinds.
Ann Moore

I have an instinct to do the wrong things. That's probably my secret. *Johann Cruyff*

This trip is a bloody shambles: the jokers, the jet-set are running this squad. You see things happening in the hotel or at training that make you want to puke. The boss is a great wee man, but he's not strong enough.
Scottish World Cup player

How can sports page cricket be so good and literary cricket so bad? And cricket is made for a musical. I can see the Cecil Beaton costumes now. *Stanley Reynolds*

Do you mean you haven't got any Jimmy Shand?
Denis Law in Norwegian record shop

Things have become so serious that unless immediate action is taken the racing industry as we know it will be gone inside two years. *Richard Baerlein*

Since I've been on the telly every night my life's not been my own. I can't even put a bet on [in a betting shop] in peace nowadays. *Joe Gormley*

We are breeding a nation of pansies.
Albert Fearnley, Bradford rugby league manager

Of course I'm against Sunday soccer. It'll spoil my Saturday nights. *John Ritchie, Stoke City*

What has happened to Crystal Palace is like watching your child take drugs. *Arthur Wait, former chairman*

Be careful, be joyful, be first.
Mr Korbut's advice to daughter Olga

The small betting-shop punter may have fun, but he can't possibly win. No chance. *John Banks*

For ageing boxers, first your legs go. Then your reflexes go. Third your friends go. *Willie Pep*

To dismiss this lad Denness you don't have to bowl fast, you just have to run up fast. *Brian Close*

Being a manager is simple. All you have to do is keep the five players who hate your guts away from the five who are undecided. *Casey Stengel, US baseball manager*

There seems only one way to beat Foreman: shell him for three days and then send the infantry in. *Hugh McIlvanney*

If Stan Bowles could pass a betting shop like he can pass a ball he'd have no worries at all.
Ernie Tagg, his manager at Crewe

Rugby is fun. Athletics hurts. *Andy Ripley*

They say some men are good putters or good chippers. Nonsense. The whole secret of golf is to choose the right club for the right shot. *Gary Player*

There's no style left in cricket, no individuality. Players should wear numbers on their backs now so you can tell them apart. *Trevor Howard*

Kite flying is as exciting as sex – and Mary Whitehouse can't ban it. *John Bally, British champion*

When John Williams, the Welsh full-back, took up rugby, he quite simply revolutionized the whole game. *Andy Irvine*

When the full story of Manchester United in recent years is told Sir Matt Busby will not be its hero. *J. L. Manning*

There are only two alternatives to taking anabolic steroids – don't take them and be second class, or give up athletics. *Howard Payne*

Three-up, three-down is ludicrous: managers are asked only two things after each game now – 'will you avoid relegation, and if so, will you get into Europe?' *Tony Waddington*

Most cricket critics, who have more power than any other writers in sport, would see Chairman Mao as British Prime Minister before they would give Boycott the vote as England's captain. *Ian Wooldridge*

The French selectors never do things by halves: for the first International of the season against Ireland they have dropped half their threequarter line. *Nigel Starmer-Smith*

Most of the ILTF are idiots – a bunch of antiquated, unresponsive, self-perpetuating septuagenarians. *Arthur Ashe*

At squash there is a fantastic and savage and unrivalled and unbelievable satisfaction at the moment you know you have beaten your opponent. There is simply no feeling on earth like it – it is a primitive thing, a conquest, an utter victory. You look into his eyes and you see the defeat there, the degradation, the humiliation, the beaten look and there isn't anything in the world like it. *Jonah Barrington*

Glasgow's violence and Scotland's shame is a surfeit of bad sex. If Scotland's football hooligans had it off before they reached the terraces they'd be less likely to reach for the nearest sharp object to stick in the opposition.

Gordon McGill

Multi-racial sport – or isolation. That seems the logical choice for South Africa. *Carwyn James*

I enjoy helming more than anything. I don't get any fun at all out of winching. *Edward Heath*

How much further down his head will Bobby Charlton have to part his hair before he faces the fact that he is bald?

Clive James

During the first Test, when Colin had no idea he'd been called for, I was waking up every few minutes to try to find out the score. I found this station that gave the total every hour, and Colin insisted that I woke him every time to tell him the score. *Mrs Penny Cowdrey*

Ali fought over the ropes as if he was leaning backwards out of the bathroom window to see if the cat was on the roof.

George Plimpton

I'd like to see a return of the wingers, the days of Matthews and Finney, Hancocks and Mullen, Huntley and Palmer, Fortnum and Mason. *Eric Morecambe*

Our decline as a football power started when boot styles changed and the wogs no longer knew what it was like to be on the receiving end of a British toecap. *Michael Parkinson*

The cult of the manager is ridiculous and embarrassing: I've had standing ovations on some grounds while the players themselves don't warrant a cheep. *Jack Charlton*

Cycling is full-pelt, high cross-winds, close formation, all pushing and shoving – it's a real he-man's sport.

Ian Hallam

I love Liverpool so much that if I caught one of their players in bed with my missus I'd tiptoe downstairs to make him a cuppa tea. *Koppite*

. . . and the crowd are encouraging referee Thomas to blow his watch. *Hugh Johns, ITV commentator*

If I'd gone to Cambridge or Oxford there'd have been no limits to what I could've achieved. *Geoffrey Boycott*

If a soccer hooligan is brought before the magistrates for a second time the label 'FA THUG' should be branded for life on his forehead. *Letter in Portsmouth Evening News*

I once asked Bob Charlton the best way to get to United's training ground and I'm still waiting for the answer.
Ted McDougall, former Manchester United footballer

When Willie John speaks, you realize you are listening to a legend. *Dick Milliken, British Lion*

The unfairest thing in golf is the two stroke out-of-bounds penalty: if you shy away and play it safe you can get by, but if you stand up and play it like a man you can be in real trouble.
Tony Jacklin

Although some footballers are in the super-tax class, it is worth pointing out that they are still, according to the Registrar-General's classification of occupations, listed in Class 4 alongside bank detectives, butlers, furriers, market gardeners, publicans and toy designers. *Maurice Yaffe*

I think caber tossing is absolutely stupid. I feel stupid doing it. *Arthur Rowe, Highland Games champion*

I have seen myself described as ashfaced hard man or, as it has been put, 'iron' man. I don't think this opinion is necessarily correct: I would say that I think, quite categorically, that I am a gentleman. *Ronald Saunders, Aston Villa manager*

Nobody likes me. And I couldn't care a goddam stuff.
Jimmy Connors

You would think that this English Test team was in a holiday camp. Their dining room has high chairs for the players' children and on mornings of tough Tests there are England's heroes popping cornflakes into their youngsters' mouths. In Brisbane and Sydney it was absurd to call these men with bats 'batsmen': they were weak-kneed impostors.
Keith Miller

1975

In a fine summer, the Australian cricketers – who had soundly beaten England in the winter – stayed behind after they had lost a pulsating one-day final against the West Indies at Lord's. Tony Greig became captain of England, for whom David Steele played heroically. Vandals damaged the wicket during the Headingley Test. Billie-Jean King won her sixth Wimbledon singles title and another veteran, Arthur Ashe, out-thought the brash young Connors. Ali beat Frazier in an outstandingly brave championship match. After a generously long honeymoon period the snipers started aiming for Don Revie.

I am not satisfied unless I am completely dictating to my opposite prop. Some people threaten me. I would rather just hit someone. I don't say things like 'That's your last warning', I just hit him and tell him that's the first warning. Then I would hit him again and keep doing it until he has stopped messing me about. *Ian McLaughlan, British Lion*

This miners' strike is ridiculous. There's tea ladies at the top of the mine who are earning more than county cricketers. Arthur Scargill ought to come down here and try bowling twenty overs. *Ray Illingworth*

Lester rarely says anything to anyone unless it's asking you about horses. But he never asks me because he knows I won't tell him. But the only way some jockeys can get anywhere with him is by telling him about what such-and-such a horse is like to ride. They're mad. I won't tell him anything. No way. Because for sure he'd pinch it. *Pat Eddery*

At Burnley, no moustaches, no sideburns, long hair discouraged . . . and four kids of 18 suspended for being caught having a drink on Christmas Eve. But when I was at Chelsea I could go through the menu, wine and all, 'phone home for hours, entertain friends, all on the club. If I run up a 2p phone call with Burnley I get the bill. Keeps your feet on the ground that, I'm telling you. *Colin Waldron, footballer*

If a fighter don't have no defence, he might as well be in a poker game with Doc Kearns without no cards. And he's gotta be mean too, mean like Victor McLaglen cleaning out a saloon in an old John Ford movie.
Al Braverman, Chuck Wepner's manager

If it was permitted I would love to play in England. Leeds I like, because I like Allan Clarke, I like his way of playing.
Johann Cruyff

Most county cricketers play the game for the life rather than the living. For them it's the motorways of England rather than the jet lanes of the world. It's sausage, egg, and chips at Watford Gap rather than vol-au-vent and small talk on the Governor-General's lawns in Barbados. *Michael Carey*

When Olga Korbut was on, the biggest cheers were coming from the public. But when Tourischeve finished, it was the competitors who were going absolutely mad.

Pauline Prestige, national coach

Mister Bastard to you.

Jimmy Connors' reply to swearing spectator

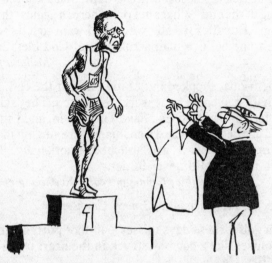

World records are like shirts. Anyone can have one if he works for it. *Filbert Bayi*

I shall continue to give relegated Luton my support – in fact I'm wearing it at this very moment. Some people think it's just the way I walk. *Eric Morecambe*

Britain's swim girls are just not tough enough. At the world championships they were no more than a glee club for the men. *Jack Queen, their coach*

I look at the First Division table and feel like trying to get in touch with God. Then I'd look at the state of our telephone exchange, and realize there was not much chance there either. *Harry Haslam, Luton Town's manager*

I've taught a young Vietnamese to swim easily, and half-castes too. Even Pakistanis do reasonably well. But Africans just sink. There is no question about it.
Chris Maloney, Gloucester swimming coach

Man, I hit Ali with punches that'd bring down the walls of a city. Lawdy, Lawdy, he's a great champion. *Joe Frazier*

It was like death. Closest thing to dyin' that I know of. I was thinking at the end 'What am I doin' here in against this beast of a man.' But after it's all over, now I want to tell the world that he's one helluva man actually, and God bless him.
Muhammad Ali

I was delirious, shocked out of my mind at the end. And to think that I had broken the world record too. They raised the Union Jack and played God Save The Queen, and I suddenly realized all the Aussies and Canadians were singing too. I had been thrilled. Now I was touched emotionally. Empire unity, a moment I'll never forget.
David Wilkie, Commonwealth swimming champion

I *am* trying for Chrissake. *Jimmy Connors*

When a golfer these days misses a 40-foot putt, he grimaces and agonizes like a cowboy struck in the heart by an Indian arrow. *Ben Hogan*

I wish I had enough money to do nothing but fly my plane, play a little golf, and go walking in woods. *Arnold Palmer*

Of the nine judges in the European championships, five came up to me afterwards and said I was the best. They had all placed me fourth. What do you say to that – or to someone who says 'You deserved to win' but then you look up what they gave you and find it was 5.7. The judging is a pain. It makes you want to spit. *John Curry, skating champion*

Husband wanted who understands nothing about football, and who will swear, when married, never to utter a single word about football. *Write Box 89, Buenos Aires Presse*

Boxing is probably the best and most individual lifestyle you can have in society without being a criminal.
Randy Neumann, US heavyweight

If you think that giving a television interview is just sitting in an armchair dressed up like a dog's dinner, drinking gin and tonic, and saying the first daft thought that comes into your head, then you're about as far off the mark as it's possible to be. *Malcolm Macdonald, Newcastle United*

At the ITV Cup final my enjoyment was considerably impaired by an occasional high-pitched whine on my television set. On ringing up to complain I was told it was Alan Ball. *Scouse Benny*

The bad facilities in Britain have created a monstrous hybrid, the neurotic pole vaulter. You have seen him, irritatingly hesitant at the end of the runway, pole nervously clenched and unclenched, fidgeting fingers being hysterically demanded elsewhere to adjust socks, shorts, and general dishevelment. Eros, the life instinct, is fighting back, arguing the case for survival in the face of folly.
Mike Bull

Keith Fletcher has been on trial longer than the late Caryl Chessman. *Alan Watkins*

I'm personally holding out for less than I'm getting.
Striking Newmarket stable lad

Epsom again fell foul of a bad referee who insisted on penalizing them for all their fouls. *Epsom and Ewell Advertiser*

Was it cosmic tragedy when somebody dug up the Test pitch with a knife and fork? Why couldn't they have moved the thing a yard or two? Elaborate explanations in *The Times* about the arcane conventions of this dotty game in no way persuade me that a just-possibly unjust prison sentence of twenty years isn't more important. *James Cameron*

G. Boycott is innocent OK. *Jon's Headingley daub*

The TV football analysts' seasonal scuffle with the English language continues: 'scores' continue to be 'scorelines', tackles to be 'scything'. The factotum adverb is still 'well" ('Hibbitt did well – didn't he do well – oh, he did do well'). If a player isn't doing well, or does something badly, he is invariably described as unlucky: 'he was very unlucky there', or simply 'oh . . . unlucky'. *Martin Amis*

Rugby players are either piano shifters or piano players. Fortunately I'm one of those who can play a tune.
                              Pierre Danos, French player

Lord Hawke probably took the same view as I do about families on tour with the MCC players. It is no more a place for them than a trench on the Somme. *John Woodcock*

The trouble with holidays is, there's plenty of places abroad, but it's finding a place that's big enough to cycle round for three weeks. I mean, Canary Isles is very nice, but it's far too small. *Beryl Burton*

My son bought a new cricket ball. On it in gold lettering it said 'Gunn and Moore Ltd., Nottingham' with 'England' added for good measure. Underneath in tiny letters, not in gold, indeed hardly visible at all, the words 'Made in India' are stamped. *Alan Watkins*

The Ann Moore engagement was a sort of sick period for me, and the court case was just awful. When you have real problems, you can go and bury yourself with your horses. They are very forgiving and comforting at times like that.
David Broome

The MCC's new tactical plan for them is to take a single in the middle of each over, so that each batsman can have a respite from the bumper barrage. *London Evening News*

There's only one head bigger than Tony Greig's – and that's Birkenhead. *Fred Trueman*

Players in Greece can earn far more selling games than winning them. Everything has a price. You don't need coaches in Greece, you need cashiers.
Joe Mallett, former Greek coach

I have always had a secret longing, far stronger than any ambition to be a Cabinet Minister, to walk out to bat in a Test match at Lord's, or still more, to play in one of the later stages on the Centre Court at Wimbledon. *Robert Carr, MP*

The crowd think that Todd handled the ball then . . . they must have seen something that nobody else did. *Barry Davies*

Just call me the promoter. Not the first black one. Not the first green one. But the promoter. There ain't no others.
Don King

If only politicians had to sweat it out to get to the Olympics they might not be quite so keen to say to we sportspeople, 'Sorry, you're not going.' *Princess Anne*

I'd rather have an accident than fall in love – that's how much I love motor racing. *Lella Lombardi, Italian driver*

What Best didn't realize until it was too late was that whereas Paul McCartney could stay up till the small hours and then write a pop song about it, George simply found it more difficult to keep himself at a level of fitness required in a top athlete. *Michael Parkinson*

The ATP stands for bans, boycotts, and baloney. They are sueing me for calling Kramer a piranha. But that's only a small fish. Get that down kid, that's an original. Any road, I'm going to expose them for the charlatans they are.

Bill Riordan, tennis entrepreneur

Since the age of 14, I have dearly wanted to be regarded as a sex object. I am absolutely sick of being loved for my cooking, accurate seam bowling, ability to solve anagrams, and obtain credit from bookmakers, and yet there are women who profess to be fearful of the alternative. *Jeffrey Bernard*

When the Amadeus String quartet play to a sold-out Festival Hall, five per cent of the audience know what it's all about – who have played quartets themselves and can empathize. When West Ham play to a sold-out Upton Park, seventy-five per cent know what it's all about. *Hans Keller*

Running for money doesn't make you run fast. It makes you run first. *Ben Jipcho*

I have one special memory of this year's Gillette. In the semifinal at Old Trafford between Lancashire and Gloucestershire . . . Foat's magnificent boundary catch to dismiss Clive Lloyd was the signal for the whole Gloucester side to descend on Foat at long leg. For David Shepherd, fielding at deep mid-on, this meant a long journey, but he set off, like a great steam engine, whistle going, flywheel spinning, rods flashing, earth shaking. Decorated, it seemed, with brass and copper, he thundered past the Railway Stand, arriving long after everyone else to shake his Foat by the hand.

John Woodcock

In an attempt to glamourize a dying industry, the sports dictionary has been turned upside down: centre forwards are strikers, throw-ins are set pieces, the pitch is now the park. In racing, grooms are calling themselves trainers, and when a horse is referred to as an in-and-out performer, it means it only wins when the stable has backed it. And a racing correspondent is now a would-be gentleman without a private income. *Jeffrey Bernard*

I am not sure that I am a good enough Davis Cup player to ever be chosen for Britain. If I get into a tight position playing for my country, I can never be sure my nerve will stand the pressure. *Mark Cox*

The rules of soccer are very simple. Basically, if it moves, kick it: if it doesn't move, kick it until it does.

Phil Woosnam, explaining the game to Americans

The singing's easy. Memorizing the words is hard.

Rocky Graziano, making his night club debut

Serenity is knowing that your worst shot is still going to be pretty good. *Johnny Miller*

Football managers don't look on county cricketers as professionals, but just because they enjoy themselves they are no less professional. There is more comradeship in cricket and nowhere near so much back-stabbing as in football. Cricketers always accept defeat, footballers cannot.

Jim Cumbes, Aston Villa and Worcestershire

I tee the ball high because years of experience have shown me that air offers less resistance than dirt. *Jack Nicklaus*

So people keep asking what it is like to win Wimbledon. Well, right after the match, when I walked off the court, they handed me a phone. Lew Hoad, who won Wimbledon twice, was on the other end. He had called from Spain midway through the final, and when he found out I was winning, he just stayed on and kept the line open till it was over. That is what it is like to win Wimbledon. *Arthur Ashe*

I did the ordinary things that ordinary managers do, like reshaping the youth scheme. But on the whole I am far above the ordinary. *Malcolm Allison*

It is not a question of dictating to Europe. If people in Britain can sit at home, and get sixty hours of TV Olympics for twenty cents – well, tell me any theatre or cinema that gives such value. *Roger Rousseau, Montreal Commissioner-General*

In Match of the Day, Jimmy Hill does his modern version of that favourite medieval theological exercise – debating how many angels could sit on the head of a pin. But with him, it's called 'Did he fall or was he pushed?' It involves slow motion, psychology, and elementary physics, and is conducted with such straight-faced fervour that it is hard to remember that he is talking of the momentary grounding of a gladiator rather than the downfall of empires. *Shaun Usher*

When television voices at the Tests do surface, it is their timbre rather than idiom which grips – a speech therapist's dream: Ray Illingworth's 'It's not a pulling wicket, this isn't', the twanging 'eows' and 'ois' that punctuate Denis Compton's carefully reclaimed accent; and Jim Laker's pronunciation is as canny as his old tweakers – if he can say swinging, why does he say innins and why doesn't he say swinnin? *Martin Amis, New Statesman*

Nastase is a Hamlet who wants to play a clown. He is no good at it. His gags are bad, his timing's terrible, and he never knows how he's going over – which last drawback is the kiss of death to any comic. *Clive James*

The Minister of Football, Mr Dennis Tharg, yesterday outlined his shock charter to combat what he called 'this malignant cancer that is destroying the name of Neasden FC'. Among the measures he proposes are: 1. Solid electric fencing 50ft high. 2. Individual observation cells to separate both fans. 3. Passports and surety of £1,000 per fan, returnable at the whistle. 4. Major laser-beam brain surgery to diminish aggressive instincts. 5. Inspector Knacker to be provided with special iron-tipped boot, capable of being brought into contact at a moment's notice with sensitive areas of the body. 6. 100-fathom deep moat, patrolled by nuclear-powered submarines and piranha sharks. *Lord Gnome*

My mother's success is akin to Germany winning the World Cup. *Mark Thatcher*

The England team to meet Australia in the first Test is: Denness, Knott, Cowdrey, Underwood, Luckhurst, Woolmer, Nicholls, Ealham, Johnson, Graham and Asif Iqbal (Hyderabad, near Beckenham, Kent): 12th Man: Fuller Pilch. *Michael Parkinson*

Every journalist who comes to see me goes away to write about 'the champion who no one knows'. What they really mean is the champion *they've* never heard of. But the 300,000 and more they get at the Grand Prix, they know who's doing what and how. *Phil Read, motorcyclist*

In the Tests I sometimes break out into a sweat just putting on me boots. You'd be really surprised at how many players are nervous out there. *Mike Hendrick*

He looked good, was good, and by golly he did us good.
Mrs Mary Chapman, farmer's wife, winning a
David Steele competition

I don't have nightmares about my team. You gotta sleep before you have nightmares.
Bep Guidolin, coach to Kansas Scouts

I run a dry boat. And over a two-day race we eat only apples or Mars. If I gave the crew even fresh-made sandwiches they'd 'protect' them in trouble. With apples or Mars they're happy to drop them at once and start pulling ropes.

Edward Heath, MP

When I was training I didn't care about nobody or nothing. And I even refused crumpet on Saturdays.

Charles Clover, former javelin thrower

Thornhill Baptists 1, Braishfield 1: Baptists started with ten men. Mick Harfield arrived late and made the eleven despite his tragic news that his wife had passed away the same morning. Everyone was stunned and at half-time two minutes silence was observed. Mick was a hero indeed to stay for the duration of the match. *Romsey Advertiser, March 20*

Fit and well: Mrs Rosina Harfield asks us to point out that last week's report of the Braishfield football match was completely untrue. She is fit and well.

Romsey Advertiser, March 27

1976

Performances by the likes of Jenner, Juantorena and Wilkie shone out of a Montreal Olympic Games beset with overbearing security and a ridiculously mushrooming budget. In a sweltering domestic summer the England cricketers were toasted and grilled by the West Indian fast bowlers. Richard Dunn survived five rounds with Ali, Bjorn Borg survived seven to win the first of a string of successive Wimbledon titles, and James Hunt took advantage of Nikki Lauda's absence through injury to win the world drivers' title. Don Revie heard the knives being sharpened.

Class in a football coach is when they finally run you out of town, to look like you're leading the parade.
Bill Battle, sacked Tennessee manager

No world-class backs have emerged in Britain since J. P. R. Williams and David Duckham in 1969. Never before this century have we gone anything like seven years without producing one player good enough to rank alongside the greatest in our heritage. *John Reason*

I am organizing an expedition to discover the whereabouts of David Coleman. For some time now the BBC have only been using repeats of his voice. No one can deny David is unique and that our children are being corrupted by the occasional use of five-letter words. If educationalists are to gain influence over BBC Sport and allow the use of good English again we will be forced into a literate Minister of Sport.
Letter in Private Eye

It is still embarrassing for me to play on the US golf circuit. Like the time I asked my caddie for a sand wedge and he comes back ten minutes later with a ham on rye.
Chi Chi Rodriguez, Puerto Rican golfer

Man's obsession with sport can be a real threat to marriage. Not a few homes have been broken on the playing fields of Eton, so much male and female libido is being invested in games. *Dr J. A. Harrington, Birmingham medical director*

There's a cold war on the women's golf circuit with we straights trying to put down the image of the lesbians. We criticize their dress, mannerisms and speech. We're losing sponsorship over it. They should go straight for the sake of all of us. *Carole Mann*

There's only one way I can get maximum security cover for the Olympics. But everyone must stay at home first.
General Roland Reid, Montreal military co-ordinator

My first 18ft vault wasn't any more of a thrill than my first clearance of 15ft or 16ft or 17ft. I just had more time to enjoy it on the way down. *Roland Carter, US pole-vaulter*

Running a marathon is just like reading a good book. After a while you're just not conscious of the physical act of reading.
Frank Shorter

The Eastern bloc judges didn't mark me down because of either technique or politics. It's just that they don't like champions whom they think are gay. *John Curry*

The reason I like those high-class Englishmen is that they sure appreciate a good horse.
Bunker Hunt, US racehorse owner

Boxing is sort of like jazz. The better it is the fewer people can understand it. *George Foreman*

Frank Clement lost the 800 simply because he was never able to get into the right position. *Ron Pickering*

I'm no good unless I hit over three hundred balls a day. You may not see me at the tournament because I practise at a different course. I tell the guys I haven't picked up a stick in weeks, but that's a bunch of bull. I'd go nuts if I didn't hit balls. *Lee Trevino*

Why did I lose? No reason, though you might like to know that I got tired, my ears started popping, the rubber came off my shoes, I got cramp, and I lost one of my contact lenses. Other than that I was in great shape.
Bob Lutz, after losing at Wimbledon

C'mon, you guys, let's try and take this thing seriously.
Ali, minutes before going out to fight Richard Dunn

I hate the bigtime, I feel the loss of close friends terribly. I have to have bouncers at my birthday parties now.

James Hunt

I was potentially quite bright at school, but when they'd be telling me about the reproduction of the spyrogyra, all I was thinking was how to get a left-back to overlap.

Malcolm Macdonald

I'd give up golf like a shot. It's just that I've got so many sweaters. *Bob Hope*

The champagne corks were certainly flying in the Selectors' Box at Lord's last night, as 112-year-old Sir Alec Douglas-Bedsocks and his wizened colleagues drank to England's moral victory in the summer's only drawn Test. 'No changes for the next Test,' he announced, 'unless of course the Grim Reaper intervenes between now and next Thursday.' Final Score: Anguilla 712-3 dec. (Calligharran 217, Underground-Conductor 163); England 49 (Steele retd. ill 23) and 25.9. *Lord Gnome*

One of the many things I like about Stracey as a world champion fighter is that he recognizes and realizes how ruthless his job must be. He wasn't above hitting Lewis low, or after the bell. *Frank McGhee*

If the law were to abolish blood sports it would create unemployment amongst the working classes. *Duke of Rutland*

Mr Tom Whattle, a Chelsea supporter, was fined £10 on Monday for sticking a hot dog up the anus of a police horse called Eileen. 'I was overcome with excitement after the match. I am a genuine animal lover,' he told the court.
Fulham Chronicle

I mean, fame's quite fun and all that, but as soon as anything goes wrong or you make a big bog of something, everyone knows about it, and that does taint it a bit.
Lucinda Prior-Palmer

Mike Smith treats us like men. He doesn't try to organize cinema outings for us. He achieves discipline in a responsible way, without instilling fear into players like Don Revie did at Leeds. *Terry Yorath, captain of Wales XI*

Brian Toss won the close . . . *Henry Blofeld, on Radio 2*

One thing I do suffer from is overconfidence. It's something I'm working on. *George Foreman*

On the day of a big motor race, a lot of people want you to sign something just before you get into your car, just so they can say they got your last autograph. *A. J. Foyt*

If the meek are going to inherit the earth, then the Oxford defence look like being land barons. *Overheard at Iffley Road*

For those of you with black and white sets, Liverpool are in the all-red strip. *David Coleman*

Sir, So the Home Secretary has no power to ban this foreign director coming here to make a film showing Jesus in the nude, drinking and lovemaking. Yet no such problem arose when the Government wanted to ban a Rhodesian cricket team. *Letter in The Daily Telegraph*

While English cricketers have laboured and lumbered and been seen to commit the elemental sin of fretting in public, the West Indies have displayed all the qualities once seen essential to the ambitious young District Commissioner.
Ian Wooldridge

The Stoke City defender has knee and thing injuries.
The Guardian

Doubles make me worried: Nastase calls me an S. O. B. every time I miss a shot, whereas Arthur Ashe just says 'Bad luck, James'. I just can't adjust to a partner. *Jimmy Connors*

All society is based on specialists. Except the decathlon. The decathlon is a presentation of moderation.
Bruce Jenner, Olympic champion

It's funny to me, why they make Montreal marathon downhill all the way?
Waldemar Cierpinski, Olympic marathon champion

Professionalism is, if you like, not having sex on Thursdays or Fridays. *Don Revie*

Johnson, at 29 a fine batsman and off-spinner, seems eminently suitable to be Kent's captain. He is a thoughtful and intelligent cricketer who must have made many followers of cricket less suspicious of the products of the London School of Economics. *Daily Telegraph leader*

I dedicate my gold medal to my mother, wherever she may be. *John-John Davies, US boxer*

The last batsman, Albeit Carefully, survived till lunch.
Hawkes Bay Gazette

Maybe now my wife will show more respect.
Vasily Alexeyev, on winning the Olympic heavyweight lifting gold medal

There's a whiff of the bazaar about the FA. An England team manager should not syndicate half-ghosted banalities; less still when they become controversial. England's shirts should not have become sold or changed. *Brian Glanville*

Occupation: Farm worker. *Franz Klammer's passport entry*

Truly, I think I could get more runs if England had some faster bowlers. *Vivian Richards*

I should have won the gold medal at Munich, but I'm glad now I only came third. I'm hard enough to live with as the bronze-medallist. With the gold I would have been impossible and I'd never have realized what a buffoon I was.

Dwight Stones, US jumper

Pascoe might have won the gold, but he simply ran out of time. *David Coleman*

I've got a Ford Pantera, a Porsche Carrera, and Mercedes Roadster, a De Tomaso Mangusta, another Porsche, another Mercedes, a station wagon, and a jeep. I guess I'm a nut about cars. I've also got a one-iron. And if I ever broke that little one-iron, that'd be the death in the family.

Johnny Miller

If Greig fell off the Empire State Building, he'd land in a passing furniture van fitted with mattresses.

England cricketer

When I play a round with the Mormon Miller, I must always remind myself never to talk about birds or booze.

Jack Newton

I was sitting alone in a train when this guy came up and put his hand on my knee. He persisted, so I whapped him one. He did not know what hit him. The police picked him up at the next station.

Janis Kerr, English women's shot-putt champion

Imaginative English rugby seems to have vanished. Let us have backs who can run. There is far too much talk of good ball and bad ball – in my opinion good ball is when you have possession and bad ball is when the opposition have it.

Dickie Jeeps, RFU president

One does tend to go on a bit about horses, doesn't one?

Princess Anne

Since giving up First Division soccer I feel like a decent human being again. We were remote. You couldn't walk around a shop in town without thinking all eyes were on you. Now when old men come up to me I want to talk about simple things, about trees and flowers. If you like I've found out what it's like to stand and stare again. I'm not particularly religious, but now I want to start going to church again and sing in the choir.

Alan Hinton, former Derby County winger

I'm the only man I reckon who's trained with the England rugby team in jeans. No time for fancy tracksuits. I suppose I don't suffer from cold legs like some I could mention.

Stack Stevens

Really, I should have brought back Moore and Greaves for the Italy match. *Don Revie*

Playing tennis makes me miss my child's birthday. But as long as the cheques keep coming in I can justify it to myself. *Mark Cox*

As cricket surges down the years, the mathematical cherish its statistics. But the literary relish its sharp Saxon vocab: drive, block, cut, glance, pull, spin, toss, lob, swing, not to mention its silly mid-offs and deep square-legs. *John F. X. Harriott*

English country gents often hunt birds and no one objected when Sheikh Zaid Ben Sultan, ruler of Abu Dhabi, decided to try his hand at the sport at his luxurious English mansion in the shires. What distressed neighbours was that he used a machine gun. *Newsweek*

Richard's not overawed by this Ali. Why, we've got far too many of these black chat merchants back 'ome in Bradford. He's right used to seeing them dance up and down Westgate with their tambourines every Saturday. *Jimmy Devanney, trainer of Richard Dunn*

Sir, I suggest that on the next occasion England play at Twickenham the following words be sung to the tune of the National Anthem: 'God Bless St George's Land/Mighty of Heart and Hand/God Bless Our Land/England's The Land We Love/Let's Give a Mighty Shove/God Save Our Land.' Inspired by this and with more practice at passing and kicking England could well start winning. Yours etc. A. R. C. Westlake, Farnham, Surrey. *Letter in Rugby World*

The thirty-three cranes rented by Montreal to complete building the Olympic site cost a million pounds more than it would have been to buy them. *Montreal Star*

How to pick a good English forward at rugby? Simply look for someone who is working his guts out in the last twenty minutes on a wet Wednesday night in an away match at Aberavon. *Dave Rollitt*

If you don't like speed, you can't get used to it. It's a nice feeling going at 85 mph, but you also remember what the car looks like when it hits a wall at that speed.
Franz Klammer, ski champion

I'm going to write a book, 'How to Make a Small Fortune in Sport'. You start with a large fortune.
Ruly Carpenter, president of Philadelphia Phillies

There's Parnham of Britain in last position. I'm afraid the conditions are so calm that they don't suit Doug Parnham; he's always at his best paddling into a headwind.
John Motson at Olympic canoeing

If I were the directors of Admiral I'd be looking for a get-out clause in the clothing contract before the England team did our product any more damage. *Michael Parkinson*

It's easier to win the Olympics than the US championships. At the Olympics you only have three Americans to beat.
Guy Drut, French Olympic hurdling champion

Women are to be excluded from the 11th annual conker championships at Oundle. Our event would be ridiculed if women competed.
Frank Elsom, chairman of the championship committee

Italy's second goal was the ultimate answer to Revie's dossiers – 'watch Causio, he is apt to leap two feet in the air as he receives a pass, sell a dummy while doing so, flick the ball past a defender with an instep and disappear with a puff of smoke.' *David Lacey*

1977

Don Revie had had enough and defected to Dubai. Ron Greenwood succeeded him. Liverpool won the European soccer Cup and Virginia Wade won Wimbledon, both to national rejoicing – and there was enough left over to go potty again over Geoffrey Boycott's hundredth hundred in his Test match return. Tony Greig introduced the world to Kerry Packer, an Australian entrepreneur, and cricket was never going to be the same again. In New Zealand the British Lions, overweighted by the successful domestic Welsh players, came a cropper.

People have been making money out of me. *Don Revie*

I have nightmares about having to become an umpire.
John Snow, cricketer

Golfer Andy North's sister, Pamela, yesterday married Mr Dick South. *UPI Report*

I like the Stylistics and the Carpenters. I also like going to the ballet, and sometimes take my mum. *Geoffrey Boycott*

Come on, we are all harlots – it is all a matter of price. How much do you fellows want? *Kerry Packer*

It says here, Mr Pele, that you have shaken hands with the Pope. I take it you are referring to Mr George Pope, the balding former Derbyshire right-hand bowler. *Bill Grundy*

I can tell you now that I'll know exactly when I want to retire; but when I reach that time I may not know. *Jack Nicklaus*

Geddes has scored: He kept his head even though he's got a cut over his right eye. *John Motson*

Football in the 1970s is very rewarding financially and can provide the opportunity to travel to almost any country in the world. *Don Revie in the Soccer Diary 1977*

Grass is out on its own. It's a way of life. I do all my own watering by hand because I like to see where it is going.
Jack Yardley, Wimbledon groundsman

Nigel Starmer-Smith had seven craps for England some years ago. *Jimmy Hill*

A *Private Eye* inquiry has unearthed disturbing facts which raise searing question marks over the head of Neasden soccer supremo, Ron Knee, 59. After years of inner turnmoil, Dollis Hill manager Bob Stockhausen has at last spoken out over his moment of shame – 'It was just before the match in the gents' toilet at the Cohen Arms, Tesco Road, when the ashen-faced mastermind approached me and said "Can I have a word with you?" ' Knee then made highly improper suggestions, Stockhausen alleges. *E. I. Addio*

I don't like to watch golf on television because I just can't stand people who whisper. *Dave Brenner, US comedian*

Sir Alf Ramsey was once a player's player and is now a gentleman's gentleman. *A. S. Lias*

The Lions make a great pack – of animals. The touring rugby side is a disgrace to its members and their homeland. There has been only one word to describe their behaviour here – disgusting! Two have urinated down stairwells, others have ripped seven hotel doors off their hinges. In another town Lions have thrown glasses, turned over tables, uncoiled water hoses and sprayed water. *New Zealand Truth*

Tottenham's merciless thrashing of Bristol Rovers wasn't really Spurs' victory as far as John Motson was concerned: all he could think of as the goals mounted was whether or not the Match of the Day record was going to be broken: at least a minor coronary seemed on the cards as his strangulated shrieks reached falsetto territories hitherto uncharted. When number nine went in I'm sure I heard something drop.

Ian Hamilton

Many times on the beach a good looking lady will say to me, 'I want to touch you.' I always smile and say, 'I don't blame you lady.' *Arnold Schwarzenegger, Mr Universe*

A good darts player who can count always beats a brilliant player who can't. *Leighton Rees, darts champion*

You just have to treat death like any other part of life.
Tom Sneva, US racing driver

My advice to my successor is to get a settled team as soon as possible and stick to it. *Don Revie*

On our Nottingham Forest team coach the radio dial always points to Radio 4, not Radio 1's pop. Show me a talented player who is thick and I will show you a player who has problems. *Brian Clough*

The proper method of playing mixed doubles is to hit the ball accidentally at the woman opponent as hard and as accurately as possible. Male players must not only retain equanimity on their side of the net, but create dissension on the other. *Art Hoppe, US writer/coach*

Try to imagine Frank Bough in utero and what do you get? Tony Gubba, of course. *Julian Barnes*

Lone yachtsman Prasantha Mukherjee was saved from the sea by British soldiers ten minutes after he sailed from Hamble to Calcutta yesterday. 'I was carrying several large sacks of curry powder and a generous quantity of Quaker Oats and lentils,' he explained, as he left hospital. 'My boat was designed for racing and the provisions weighed her down.' The rescue operation cost £80,000. 'It is our job to save human life,' said an Army spokesman. *Evening Express*

Exchange in Rome court: Italian prosecutor – 'You are charged with being drunk and disorderly last night, how do you plead?' Liverpool supporter – 'Liverpool Magico!' Case dismissed.

The trainer, Jeremy Tree, quizzed Lester Piggott hard one day. 'I've got to speak to the boys of my old school, Lester, and tell them all I know about racing. What shall I say?' The jockey paused and then gave a short muffled reply: 'Tell 'em you've got flu.' *Tony Lewis*

If you hadn't been there it wouldn't have been much of a fight. *Harry Carpenter to Ken Norton*

A jump jockey's got to throw his heart over the fence and then get over and catch it. *Dick Francis*

Mr Thomas Haycock, a goalkeeper, has been dropped from Greentown BMF XI after their failure to win a match in four seasons of 'uphill football'. Mr Haston Lash, Greentown's manager, said yesterday: 'Haycock's game fell to pieces after the team began calling him 'Cheesecake'. I know that he weighs 20 stone and that top-of-the-net work upsets him. Nevertheless, he has let in 107 goals in three matches.' Mr Haycock said: 'Why blame me? If the team worked together I would have nothing to do. Instead they began to call me 'cheesecake' when the ball was flashing around me. We were only losing 17–0 at half-time. They gave up too easily.' Before leaving the club house he said he would do his utmost to regain his place. *Christopher Logue, Yorkshire Post*

My golf game's gone off so much that when I went fishing a couple of weeks ago my first cast missed the lake.

Ben Crenshaw

He had always been a man to bear misfortune with stoical endurance. A racehorse owner for the past twenty years, he had his first winner – Goblin – only three weeks ago.

Sunday Telegraph

I was so impressed with Mr Boycott's conduct on your show on Saturday that I intend writing to the Director-General asking if we can see more of Geoffrey on our screens in future. And less of you. *Letter to Michael Parkinson*

Nastase's new contract is 35 pages long and 15 of those are devoted to penalties about his behaviour.

Jerry Buss, manager of the Los Angeles Strings

Even now a team of linguists is at work translating Don Revie's writings on the game from the original gibberish into Arabic. *Michael Parkinson*

I used to stand up and glare around when fans were giving Geoff stick and they all used to shout: 'Wasn't me, Mrs Hurstie, wasn't me . . . ' Geoff told me again and again to hold my tongue. Norman Hunter's mum used to lash out with her handbag when people booed her Norm.

Mrs Geoff Hurst

One day I had breakfast with the Queen. She was fantastic to talk racing with, but I was even more nervous than when I rode in the Oaks. We had scrambled eggs and tea. 'I do like tea to be tea,' she said, which means she likes it to be strong.

Willie Carson, jockey

He's going for the pink – and for those of you with black and white sets, the yellow is behind the blue.

Ted Lowe, ITV snooker commentator

A leading American football player was asked on television whether he preferred Astroturf or grass. He replied, 'I don't know, man, I've never smoked Astroturf.' *Tim Fell*

Kuwait has placed an order with a British firm to supply 25,000 footballs – but stipulated that they must be delivered inflated. Mercury International, of Longton, said they would ship out the balls deflated to save cargo space, but would send out a special team to blow the things up after unloading. *Reuter report*

Remember, postcards only, please. The winner will be the first one opened. *Brian Moore, ITV*

The ideal soccer board of directors should be made up of three men – two dead and the other dying. *Tommy Docherty*

At the end I couldn't hear what the Queen was saying to me. But it was just great to see her lips moving. *Virginia Wade*

Sports pages of the popular press are still woefully old-fashioned. Numerous talented sports journalists on popular papers in Fleet Street might as well check in their perceptions, their originality, and their seriousness at the front desk for all the use they'll be allowed to make of them.

Brian Glanville

Rose's brain will now be telling him exactly what to do.

Ron Pickering

There have been various occasions since he became an England cricketer when Greig has overplayed his hand . . . what has to be remembered of course is that he is not an Englishman by birth or upbringing, but only by adoption. It is not the same thing as being English through and through.

John Woodcock, The Times

To the world at large, the little grey-haired lady looks like everyone's idea of the perfect librarian. But beneath the calm bookish appearance of Mrs Anne Evans, Aberystwyth librarian, there beats a passionate heart. She has a secret love. For Mrs Evans is such an Arsenal fanatic that she even arranges the books on her shelves so that the covers make a bank of red and white. On match days she too always wears red and white clothes – though she also changes her outfit to yellow and blue when Arsenal have to wear their away strip. *Sunday People*

Cricket is a situation game. When the situation is dead, the game is dead. *Trevor Bailey*

I don't seem to use my intelligence intelligently.
Virginia Wade

For a footballer, it's like living in a box. Someone takes you out of the box to train and play . . . and makes all your decisions. I have seen players, famous internationals, in an airport lounge all get up and follow one bloke to the lav. Six of them maybe, all standing there not wanting a piss themselves, but following the bloke who does. *Geoff Hurst*

Of the three Yorkshiremen who have scored 100 hundreds, the most beautiful player, by far, was Hutton. The man to play an innings for your life was Sutcliffe. The man to play an innings for his own life is Boycott. *Alan Gibson*

I asked Ron Knee how he saw the future now his side had not qualified. 'We must start again from scratch,' he said. 'Throw out the dossiers, and concentrate on essentials like equipping the squad with proper spectacles and deaf aids so they are fully responsive to each others position off the ball at any given moment in time. *E. I. Addio*

The Irish hammer thrower, Bernie Hartigen, was warming up in the Europa Cup at Copenhagen yesterday. On his first throw his sixteen-pound hammer smashed a new installed photo-timing system, hit an official on the head and missed the judges' table by inches. *Daily Mail*

Ninety per cent of baseball is half mental.
Jim Wohlford, Milwaukee Brewers outfielder

There are two separate women's swimming championships, one for East Germans, one for the rest. You only have to listen to their voices to know why. One of the girls in my squad complained that there were men in the women's changing room at a recent international gala in Vienna, only for the chaperone to discover on investigation that she had merely overheard East German girls in the next cubicle.
Charles Wilson, British swimming coach

The sumptuous and singular footballistic stage which is under construction at Mar del Plata has now reached 75 per cent of its total erection.
Argentine World Cup Organizing Committee

Look at that tremendous flexibility of the ankles. They really are an extension of the legs.
Ron Pickering, gymnastics commentator

In his century at Headingley, Boycott touched the ankle of his right foot 40 times each hour. He took off his cap and wiped his brow 364 times. He played 466 balls. He marks his guard twice every time he gets down to the business end, one at the usual mark, the other inside of his crease.
Jack Fingleton

There are only two basic situations in football. Either you have the ball or you haven't. *Ron Greenwood*

They call women's pro golf the Bitchy Bitch circuit: it's more like the Butchy Butch. They don't seem to have separate dinner dates or anything. They all stick together in their groups and if two of the girls who've paired off have a row, the atmosphere is terrible. *Julie Welch*

Woman is Sheep Dog Champion. *Guardian headline*

1978

The World Cup was won by the host nation, Argentina, three of whose squad at once joined English clubs. The exploits of the bedraggled Scottish side hogged most domestic headlines. Liverpool retained the European Cup. Daley Thompson and Steve Ovett were notable athletics successes, and Jack Nicklaus, the universal favourite, won the Open golf title. Yorkshire sacked Boycott as captain; Derby County retained Tommy Docherty for a while as manager even though he admitted lying to the High Court, and the astonishing Muhammad Ali first lost his heavyweight title to Leon Spinks and then regained it for an unprecedented third time.

Boycott might be the harder man to get out, but I have never known it suggested that anyone in his own side has deliberately run Brearley out. *Alan Gibson*

When Nicklaus plays well, he wins. When he plays badly, he's second. When he plays terrible, he's third.
Johnny Miller

It's one thing to ask your bank manager for an overdraft to buy 500 begonias for the borders in Haslemere, but quite another to seek financial succour to avail oneself of some of the 5-2 they're offering on Ile de Bourbon for the St Leger.
Jeffrey Bernard

I was unable to collect my £91,000 ITV Seven winnings from the bookmaker because I couldn't find the time: I was so busy on the allotment, and also had to feed my chickens, that I couldn't fit it in. *Frank Bradley, assistant seedsman*

I play squash twice a week, and jogging round Wimbledon Common is a great joy. One day I sighted three nuns ahead, so turned off on to a side path only to run into three people I knew. Also, I never miss Match of the Day.
Cardinal Basil Hume

Sir – I think it is degrading and slightly vulgar for you to print news about football on the front page of your paper. Yours etc., J. G. Riddall, Leeds 7. *Letter in The Guardian*

At Crystal Palace the BBC cameras picked up a solemn lady called Paula Fudge as she pounded along a running track with BRITISH MEAT written across her understandably heaving bosom. Sponsorship in sport is one thing but this was altogether a different kettle of offal. *Dennis Potter*

I felt ashamed for myself and Scotland, but I do not think that some of the Scottish team have the brains to feel ashamed. *Martin Buchan*

Gower is a different class. His bat is such an extension of his arms and wrists that the blade often appears to be flexible.
H. F. Ellis

The world of soccer was rocked to its foundations yesterday when an ashen-faced Ron Knee, 59, broke down and told a High Court judge that everything he had said was 'a pack of lies in the strictly legal sense of the phrase'. His tight lips trembling for the first time in living memory, the controversial Neasden supremo told the jury, 'I did not lie deliberately. It just came natural.' Later, following a showdown meeting, club chairman, Brig. Buffy Cohen, said: 'We are standing behind Big Ron 100 per cent. Ron told me at the outset he was an incompetent drunken liar and every word he said is true.'

E. I. Addio, Our Man in the Visitor's Gallery with
the Yorkie Bar and the Sporting Life

When Daley Thompson was winning all those events at Edmonton everyone in our house was cheering like mad at the telly. *Viv Anderson, black footballer*

After enjoying Ipswich winning the Cup Final Mrs Thatcher was asked on Radio 2 who was her Man of the Match. Without hesitation she replied 'The Number Ten shirt, Trevor Whymark'. Her erring staff had neglected to point out to her that though Whymark was listed in the programme, he was in fact injured and did not play. *Daily Mail*

'I had never seen such a display of dancing in the ring,' said Mr Big-Toe Dankovitch, trainer to Harvey Gartley. 'I told Harvey to dance in the first round, sure enough Oulette never landed a punch. But Harvey overdid it. He danced himself into exhaustion and collapsed unconscious after 47 seconds. Oulette won on a technical knockout.'

Christopher Logue, South China Post

Umpires at Wimbledon seem to take pleasure in ignoring the pathetic gesticulating Nastase when he asks them to explain their rather dubious decisions. Why is it part of an umpire's duties to treat a fellow being with such contempt? I suppose that umpires, whose duties seem to consist principally of saying 'Thirtay, fortay' and things like that, have to cultivate feelings of self-importance to make their business seem worthwhile. *Alexander Chancellor*

In reply to your question, What is always brought to Cup finals but never used? (the loser's ribbons that are tied to the cup), the answer should surely be 'Malcolm Macdonald'.
Laurence Lebor, letter in The Guardian

At the end of 'La el darem la mano', the famous Don Giovanni duettino, the music, now in a rather speedy siciliano rhythm, virtually turns into its opposite; unity is achieved by a complementary contrast. Let that master be my model for a concluding tribute to another master of wordless logic – West Ham's Trevor Brooking at Upton Park on Saturday. *Hans Keller, Spectator*

Sir, You state that Brooke Bond Oxo is using Mrs Ally MacLeod in advertisements for tea. This is not so. We use chimps to promote our world cup. Yours etc. D. F. Barnett, Deputy Managing Director. *Letter in The Guardian*

'I caught them in the act when I flung back the curtains,' said Mrs Juniper Masters, of Carshalton. Denying that he had been adulterous with his dancing partner, Carole Croxley, Mr Robert Masters said: 'I had moved the snooker table into the bedroom for greater elbow room. The noise my wife heard was merely an expression of my delight at having potted the black. The same excitement accounts for the fact that my wig was askew. As for why Miss Croxley had her trousers off – well, she had split the side seam while executing a backhand shot only a few moments before Juniper made her astonishing entry.
Christopher Logue, The Daily Telegraph

C'mon the Whites! *Bored cricket watcher*

Sir, The record for the greatest number of symbols added to or removed from the weather map in a single forecast for so long held by that great stalwart, Jack Scott, was broken by Michael Fish in November, 1977. He increased the score from 7 to an unheard of 11 . . . but now Bill Giles has scored an unequivocal 14 in the late evening forecast which must surely have ensured his place for the Commonwealth Games. Yours etc., Peter M. Williams, Merthyr Tydfil.
Letter in The Guardian

Nothing can be wholly bad, even football . . . a girl told me that football on the telly was driving her up the wall. In anguish she tried BBC2 to be greeted by a film in Swedish with letters along the bottom. Finally she had to resort to a desperate remedy to fill the aching vacuum. She went to bed with a book. So the World Cup may yet trigger off an astonishing revival in the art of the novel. *John Mortimer*

And umpire Dickie Bird is gestating wildly as usual.
Tony Lewis, BBC

This dolphin effect can lead to a sinking situation and might even produce a drowning problem.
Jim Railton, BBC, on the Boat Race

When we were living in Sydney a friend told me that one night, while she and her husband were making love, she suddenly noticed something sticking in his ear. When she asked him what it was he replied 'Be quiet! I'm listening to the cricket.' *Vicky Rantzen, The Observer*

If, as every Englishman suspects, the Scots ingest a weakness for hyperbole with their mother's milk, Ally MacLeod would seem to have been breast-fed until he was fifteen.
Hugh McIlvanney

When Randall was run out backing-up in New Zealand I thought that if that had been my school the bowler would have been beaten for it by a housemaster – and quite right too. *Phil Edmonds*

During the course of Wimbledon, Dan Maskell said 'Ooh I say' a total of 1,358 times. The trouble with Dan's style is that it's so infectious. Ooh I say, it's a really infectious style.
Clive James

When I left Yorkshire I received a letter from the secretary saying they were not going to offer me a contract which began: 'Dear Ray Illingworth . . .' But they had crossed the 'Ray' out. They couldn't even bring themselves to call me by my first name or use a fresh piece of paper. *Ray Illingworth*

Police were searching Eastbourne last night for a middle-aged woman who stabbed Big Bruno Elrington, the 6ft, 16 stone Portsmouth heavyweight wrestler, who had been thrown out of the ring by his opponent. She thrust a knitting needle into his back before fleeing the hall. Mr Elrington went to hospital for injections. *The Times*

The world of soccer was rocked to its foundations last night by the news that Neasden soccer supremo Ron Knee, 59, had clinched a multi-million pound deal to buy Argentine-born Hernandez de les Pretwinkle, 46. Ashen-faced Knee told the press: 'How did I do it? Simple. I tracked him down to a hairdressing salon in Tescoe Road and made him an offer he couldn't refuse, to wit a life's supply of Boston's Rio de Janeiro, Junta-style Knockout Stout.'
E. I. Addio, Our Man in the Books and Mags shop
with Dark Glasses

Sure I eat what I advertise. Sure I eat Wheaties for breakfast. A good bowl of Wheaties with Bourbon can't be beat.
Dizzy Dean, US athlete

At Ascot today the heat is quite hot. *Judith Chalmers, BBC*

For the capacity to enliven a dull game, to bring a sleepy public to life; for bouts of furious, violent athleticism channelled through control, and interspersed with spells of amusingly haughty impassivity: for taking the whole thing as seriously as his watchers want him to, but not a touch of anguish more – I think it would be hard to beat the cricketer, Viv Richards. *Russell Davies*

Not since Betty Grable has so much been written about a pair of legs as John Lloyd's. Nastase's agent told me, in a fit of jealousy, that he hopes Lloyd gets varicose veins. *Taki*

Modern players all carry an attaché-case with a hair dryer in it. And they've all got headphones. You've got to book three seats on a plane for every two ballplayers so they can put their hi-fis and hair dryers down.
Cal Griffith, Minnesota Twins' owner

Whoever stole it is spending less money than my wife.
Illie Nastase, on failure to report theft of his American Express card

I'm sorry I did not win a gold medal at Prague as expected. This was because (a) I felt exhausted after Edmonton, (b) I was not taking drugs like everyone else; (c) British athletics are so badly organized; (d) I am building up for Moscow '80; (e) I could not live up to my Golden Boy press tag; (f) I had this terrible hangover; (g) I am waiting for the right girl to come along. *Miles Kington*

Thursday: Mudassar, given lbw, was furious when he returned to the changing-room. He said: 'That's the end of cricket for me. I think I'll start running a discotheque.'
Wasim Bari's diary, quoted by Dudley Doust, The Sunday Times

A nun, Collette Duveen, of the Order of the Merciful Sisters, was arrested for kicking in the teeth of a lorry driver who cheered when Holland scored their second goal in the World Cup final. *News of the World*

I think it is a happy coincidence that the ball is the instrument of the sport represented by FIFA. It is round without angles or sharp edges. With its unlimited surface, lines may criss-cross to infinity. When in motion it can be impelled in all directions with no deformation and without losing its characteristics. To fulfil its performance it is necessary never to be still, always on the move. I feel you can take it as a symbol of my work as your president of FIFA.

Joao Havelange

Ron Pickering continued to overheat as usual. The mockery of my confreres had chided him out of saying 'he's pulling out the big one', and even 'he's whacking in the big one'; but the National Viewers' and Listeners' Association will cut off his tail with a carving knife for his new and shameful variant: 'If she hits the board and bangs a big one, that'll put her in the bronze medal position.' *Julian Barnes, New Statesman*

I resigned as a coach because of illness and fatigue. The fans were sick and tired of me. *John Ralston, Denver Broncos*

Ted Heath is the Geoff Boycott of politics – he doesn't like to play unless he can be captain. But the comparison is unfair to Boycott. In the first place Boycott in many ways is a modest and unassuming man. In the second, he has a great loyalty to his county. And in the third, he makes a hell of a lot of runs. Heath rarely makes any runs, and always ends knocking down all his stumps. *Paul Johnson*

CBK—7**

I'll chase that son of a bitch Borg to the ends of the earth. I'll be waiting for him. I'll dog him everywhere. Every time he looks round he'll see my shadow. *Jimmy Connors*

There's been a colour clash; both teams arrived wearing white. *John Motson*

To put it very simply, spelt out virtually in words of one syllable: Hunt Servants are the salt of the earth. At all times and in all conditions they do their best to provide us with sport. Whether they get a Christmas box or not, there is no thought of their going on strike.

Loriner, Horse and Hound columnist

Four minutes to half-time; one-one; whoever scores now will go in with an advantage. *Hugh Johns, ITV*

Watching the Beeb is something deeper, something occult, something to do with David Coleman's personality. Just by being so madly keen, he helps you get things in proportion. Anything that matters so much to David Coleman, you realize, doesn't matter so much at all. *Clive James*

Graves is likely to be out for a month with a broken index finger on his bottom hand. *Robin Marlar, The Sunday Times*

Ted Dexter is to journalism what Danny La Rue is to Rugby League. *Michael Parkinson*

Our problem is that we've tried to score too many goals.
Gordon Lee, Everton manager

Those athletes who have been here in Edmonton for five or six days are beginning to open out their legs and show their form. None have shown it better than a Scotsman and an Englishwoman. *Chris Brasher, The Observer*

I was vaguely startled to read in a British travel magazine the other day that it would be a good idea 'to explore the unknown parts of Rodney Marsh'. When I re-read the passage it had changed mysteriously to 'the unknown parts of Romney Marsh'. *Miles Kington*

Why are the umpires, the only two people on a cricket field who aren't going to get grass stains on their knees, the only ones allowed to wear dark trousers? *Katharine Whitehorn*

Stopping otterhunting is unlikely to benefit otters
The Field

Handy phrases: Dejen de torturarme, por favor (Please stop torturing me). Mi periodico les pagara bien si me dejen ir (My newspaper will pay well if you let me go). Por favor entregen mi cuerpo a mi familia (Please deliver my body to my family). *NUJ handbook to journalists covering World Cup*

I'd give my right arm to get back into the England team.
Peter Shilton, goalkeeper

If Borg nips about the Centre Court with Brillo pads under his arms, who cares? But if, at Virginia's dynamic serve, the cameras zoom in on a hairy female armpit, Wimbledon would never be the same again. *Val Hennessy, Evening News*

Standing still is the same as going backwards, and when you do that people are bound to overtake you.
Ian Wolstenholme, Harlow FC manager

Retire? Retire to what? I already fish and play golf.
Julius Boros, golfer

If a player's ball lies in a mortar shell crater he may move it without penalty. *Notice at Hillside Golf Club, Umtali*

If those West Ham defenders weren't sleeping, they were certainly slumbering. *John Motson*

I am convinced that Laurie Cunningham is the greatest talent we have ever seen in this country, and I include Stan Matthews and George Best.
George Petchey, Millwall manager

In Mike Brearley's unarrogant flat, where he lives alone – rumpled bedclothes in mid-afternoon and unwashed plates on the kitchen table – I made a beeline for the bookshelves. I spotted *Games People Play, The Divided Self, Human Aggression, The Art of Loving, Perspectives in Group Therapy, The Miracle Worker, The Poems of Auden.* I wonder what books Greig and Boycott have on their shelves?
David Benedictus

If I were a grouse I'd appeal to the Brace Relations Board.
Jilly Cooper

I only took two tablets. *Willie Johnston, Scottish footballer*

They're selling video cassettes of the Ali-Spinks fight for $89.95. Hell, for that money Spinks will come to your house.
Ferdie Pacheco

Not since he once wished viewers a Happy Yew Near has Frank Bough ever quite said precisely what he means.

Dennis Potter

I'm glad to say this is the first Saturday in four weeks that sport will be weather-free. *David Coleman*

It was Ludwig Wittgenstein who first made me interested in cricket when he said in the *Logico-Absurdicus* that 'everything of which we cannot speak is a lot of balls', said Mike Borely, England's captain. 'When I am waiting for Lillee to bowl I find myself humming the second subject from the Adagio furioso third movement of Haydn's opus 74 string quartet, better known to music lovers as 'the Duck', which is what I usually score.' *Lord Gnome*

I went to a fight last night and an ice hockey game broke out.

Rodney Dangerfield, comedian

. . . and so to 1979 . . .

I am far more interested in young Arsenal goalkeepers than in myself. *Bob Wilson, part-time soccer coach*

Not that I'd ever think of leaving 'ere. I love England. But I do resent giving the Income Tax inspector 83 per cent. I tell him he's welcome to it if he went out and got on my bike and got throwed up the road at 190 mph, be in hospital for weeks, then walk around 'alf crippled for the rest of his life . . . If they did that they're welcome to my money. *Barry Sheene*

It's hard to get casual workers in skiing these days. Kids just aren't dropping out like they used to.
Dick Elias, Colorado entrepreneur

When I was dropped by Spurs it hurt deep down; just like being kicked in the teeth. *Neil McNab*

The only hope for the England rugby union team is to play it all for laughs. It would pack them in if the public address system at Twickenham was turned up full blast to record the laughs at every inept bit of passing, kicking or tackling. The nation would be in fits . . . and on the telly the BBC would not need a commentator but just a tape of that 'Laughing Policeman', turning it loud at the most hilarious bits.
Jim Rivers, letter in The Guardian

Sir Harold Thompson, chairman of the FA, treated me like an employee. These Arab Sheikhs treat me like one of them.
Don Revie

You cannot sustain top championship golf if you're longing for home and the kids every time you walk up some foreign fairway. *Johnny Miller*

We are delighted with a dozen or so good youngsters in English soccer. We should be talking about hundreds. We give away coaching badges, willy nilly, to people not qualified even in basics. Some of our young players are still sweeping the terraces. Some First Division managers do not even know the names of their apprentices. *Ron Greenwood*

The all-white suits of this German ski team make them look so very colourful. *Emlyn Jones ITV commentator*

Red Rum will run in no more Grand Nationals. For one thing he has no time. He opens supermarkets now at £1,000 a time, or launderettes, or pubs . . . and if not he's at home replying to his fifty letters a week, twenty poems and even some telegrams, or producing the manure that is packed and raffled for charity. *Press release*

The era of the manager talking for a fighter is over. If managers aren't going to do the fighting then they shouldn't be doing the talking. *Sugar Ray Leonard*

RENTAJOGGER – only $1.95. Rent me and I will jog for you at least one mile a day (weather permitting) for the next year. *Ad in New York Times*

Evans, a Welsh international, was fined for alleged misbehaviour in the Embassy World Championships and has appealed. The appeal is due to be heard on Saturday and local farts fanatics will be hoping for a happy outcome.
Oldham Evening Chronicle

I don't mind starting the season with unknowns. I just don't like finishing the season with them.
Lou Holtz, Arkansas Football club

Nobody ever beats Wales at Rugby, they just score more points. *Graham Mourie, New Zealand captain*

I have had a lot of barracking about my homemade batting helmet. When it fell off at Trent Bridge a cousin of D. Randall shouted 'Eh, Brearley, why don't y'pin it on with a six-inch nail!' *Mike Brearley*

My youngest son and I were intrigued by your article on the childhood of Trevor Francis. Mr Francis has obviously forgotten those impeccable manners, for when my son politely asked for his autograph on Saturday, February 3, after the Chelsea v. Birmingham match, the footballer's reply was 'Piss off!' *Mrs Nora Prestcott, letter in The Guardian*

£8,000 FACELIFT FOR WESTERHAM SPORTS-WOMEN *Sevenoaks News*

This change of venue will give the Desert Classic a much better chance of being as good as it always has.
Labron Harris, USPGA tournament organizer

Whatever the irritations of his frequent bouts of ranting, his weird pastiche of philosophies that often give the impression of embracing anything from Bevanite Socialism to Zen Buddhism, and the declaratory eccentricity of his behaviour, it is impossible not to wish Brian Clough well. Two of him would be a crowd, but the one we have should be enjoyed.
Hugh McIlvanney

England batsmen will never get many runs if they persist in sitting on their back foot. *Sir Len Hutton*

If you run marathons and don't smoke, it is absolutely impossible to have a heart attack. *Dr Jack Scaff*

When reporters ask if sex before a fight affects my performance, I always say 'which performance?' *John Conteh*

Tennis is a game where you give other people a chance to lose to you. We all hate the dinker, but he understands the definition best; at every level right up to Harold Solomon the dinker will win because he has a higher intellectual principle, a higher frustration-tolerance threshold, and a longer concentration span. *Jack Kramer*

In Spain, when little, the other caddies sat playing boy's games and laughed when my brother Sevvy came in – how you say? – like a drowning rat maybe five hours afterwards. They no laugh today. They still carry golf bags.
Manuel Ballesteros

When the car somersaulted at 280 mph when I was going for the record, my only thought was 'God, the wife is going to kill me for this.' *Barry Bowles*

If the good Lord had ever shown me how to pick out the googly from a leg-break at a range of about twenty yards I would not now be a sportswriter. *Ian Wooldridge*

I try to keep myself in the best of company and my horses in the worst of company. *Lenny Goodman, jockeys' agent*

Thank you, Jimmy Hill.
> *Russell Harty, after half-hour ITV interview with*
> *Jimmy Greaves*

JOG HELPS SNOG *Grafitti in London gym*

There is an unwritten law in rugby that you never tread on the head of a player if you can avoid it. *Chris Ralston*

After being refused renewal of a firearms licence 'for intemperate behaviour' by Judge Lloyd Jones, Dr Robert Arkle, 56, said he had won many shooting tournaments over three decades. 'Alcohol tightens up the eyeball, keeps it more round, makes the vision better and relaxes you,' he said. 'Some people take tranquilizers. I happen to drink a lot. *Sports Illustrated*

My John (Lloyd) is such a gent. He always thinks about other people. I think most British people are like him. *Chris Evert*

I am suffering from the ridiculous delusion that I cannot putt. *Tony Jacklin*

The new Polish midfield player called Ritchie Duda made such an impressive debut for Chicago Sting that by half-time his colleagues had nicknamed him 'Zippitty'.
> *New York Herald Tribune*

Like a hole-in-one at golf, a maximum snooker break can only ever be an aimed-for fluke. *John Spencer*

EX-BOXER BATTERED OUTSIDE CHIP SHOP
> *Cheltenham Echo*

At times Boycott could get bogged down to such an extent that his only way out was to call for and run desperate singles without reasonable regard for his partner's safety. Furthermore, the temptation to concentrate the strike on himself in favourable conditions was not always resisted.
Richard Hutton

I did not particularly mind the photographers when I was actually riding – it was how the wretched men kept getting in the way beforehand that bothered me. *Princess Anne*

Alan Ball loves his wife, adores his kids, is totally unselfish, misunderstood, wildly generous, moody, patriotic and loyal.
Lawrie McMenemy

Brearley did more in Australia than achieve a triumph for himself. He illuminated the art of captaincy, which has always been a part of cricket. I do wish, though, that he would do something to curb the kissing at even the simplest catch. *Alan Gibson*

I am coming back to Britain. I would rather be poor and happy. *Sue Barker*

It's a perfect day here in Australia – glorious blue sunshine.
Christopher Martin-Jenkins, BBC radio

Ben Crenshaw has the best grip, the best stance and the best swing I've ever seen. Besides that, he's nice. *Lee Trevino*

What Liverpool have here is the atmosphere of everyone being involved, togetherness, like a family. It's like your brother, if your brother's in a bit of trouble you help him, don't you? Well, if your mate is in a bit of trouble on the pitch you help him too. They try it at other clubs, but Liverpool just have the knack of doing it better. *John Toshack*

Chris Evert is one of the best jokesters on the circuit. And the most popular. It's impossible not to like Chris.
Julie Heldman

You can almost hear the crowd's audible sigh of relief.
Bill McLaren, BBC

Putting is the absolute key to golf. It can erode the whole fabric. It's ruined my iron play for a long time now because I've been trying to push irons too near the pin to compensate; and once that starts you start straining off the tee; and once that starts you might as well stay home and watch movies.

Arnold Palmer

Whenever I shake hands with Gareth Edwards I wish he could have been my brother. *Cliff Morgan*

The satisfactions of a day's fishing are deep; and just as deep on a day when you don't catch a fish; but unless you keep faith that you are going to catch a fish that day, then fishing seems a waste – a waste of time, money, effort and, most depressing, spirit. Few things can make a man feel more fully a man than fishing, if he has got faith; nothing can make a man more fully a fool if he has not got faith.

William Humphrey

C'mon Brearley, f'Gawd'sake, you make Denness look like Don Bradman. *Sydney barracker*

After a recent TV interview the Yankee's coach, Yogi Barra, was given a cheque for $100. The cheque read 'Pay to Bearer'. Yogi examined it and said to the interviewer, 'Come on, you've known me long enough to know how to spell my name.' *Sports Illustrated*

At Oxford C. B. Fry's party trick was to leap backwards from carpet to mantelpiece from a standing fart.

The Guardian (first edition)

At Oxford C. B Fry's party trick was to leap backwards from carpet to mantelpiece from a standing tart.

The Guardian (second edition)

At Oxford C. B. Fry's party trick was to leap backwards from carpet to mantelpiece from a standing start.

The Guardian (third edition)

The slalom champion, Stenmark, does not ski downhill.

Frank Bough, BBC

In the Mansfield incident, the court heard, Robson ran onto the pitch and took down his trousers. He then removed his underpants, bent forward and showed his backside to the crowd. Judge Gerrard commented: 'It might be possible for a football club to take photographs of people like this and refuse them admittance to the ground.'

Stafford Evening Sentinel

Ricky Wilson, 18, was fined £400 for throwing one peanut at the match. Said Birmingham Magistrate, Clyde Riley, 'It doesn't matter what he threw. Things don't have to be heavy to cause injury.' *Birmingham Mail*

There are three reasons I can be wicketkeeping badly . . . lack of concentration, standing up too soon, or snatching at the ball. The longer you stay crouching, even for a thousandth of a second, may mean the difference between the ball glancing off your finger or sticking to the middle of your glove. *Bob Taylor*

When the team raised eyebrows at my language I said 'I'm the new coach, not the new Pope'.

Dick Versace, US basketball trainer

109

Footballers can never be truly objective about their performances, but Nottingham Forest are at least much less readily carried away than most. They recognize the vital, often obscured boundaries that separate pride from vanity and dissatisfaction from resignation. *Hugh McIlvanney*

JPR Collides with Road Tanker – the Tanker Spent a Comfortable Night in Hospital and is Expected to Recover.
Title of poem by Tom Bellion

If the Russians beat America at ice hockey they go home and are rewarded with better conditions, like a home that has two light bulbs instead of one. If America win, it doesn't matter for the players are making so damn much anyway, like the average wage for an NHL player is nearly $50,000.
Harold Ballard, Toronto Maple Leafs

Kerry Packer has made lifelong friends turn into enemies.
Jeff Stollmeyer, West Indies cricket official

An amateur soccer player whose toupee slipped during a game sued its manufacturer in a Welsh court, claiming he had suffered pain and embarrassment. The judge was told that when Norman Bollard, a thirty-two-year-old butcher from Overton, headed the ball, it pushed his "dream head of hair" over his eyes. On hearing the laughter of the other players, he ripped up the toupee on the spot. The manufacturers agreed to an out-of-court settlement of £355, the only condition being that Bollard gave them back the pieces.
Sports Illustrated

I peak every time I play. *Jimmy Connors*

If John has to diet, then I have to diet. If he can't eat ice-cream then nor can I. If it's steak and cabbage, same for me. I run with him in the mornings and exercise with him on the living-room floor. For seven weeks before his last fight I slept every night next to him in the same bed, but never once could we . . . well you know . . . *Mrs John L. Gardner*

I can handle fame, because I've seen it coming all along.
Daley Thompson

If England asked Kevin Keegan to sail singlehanded round Cape Horn he would do it with pleasure. *Bill Shankly*

In the Boat Race, if an oarsman ever thinks about his girl-friend for one moment, the thing would be lost. They must never even look at the other boat. Our tiny craft holds nine bodies, but more important nine minds. All day they've got to think of themselves as ruthless bloody executioners. They've each got to have their opposite number's balls in their hand and squeeze them till they can stand it no longer.
Daniel Topolski, Oxford's coach

Against Connors and Borg you feel like your being hit with a sledgehammer. But this guy McEnroe has a stiletto; he just slices you up. He has a ton of shots – a slice here, a nick there, a cut over here. Pretty soon you've got blood all over you, even though the wounds aren't deep. But very soon you've bled to death. *Arthur Ashe*

QUIZ: What is the most popular sport in Britain today – a) darts; b) fishing; c) betting; d) travelling on the Tube with-out a ticket; e) sports' quizzes; f) making up remarks sup-posed to have been said by David Coleman? *Miles Kington*

Jimmy (Connors) always had to hate the men players to be at his best. But they don't hate him back any more. A lot of them like him now. So it's very hard for him to find new motivation. *Chris Evert*

111

In south-west Lancashire, babes don't toddle; they sidestep. Queuing women talk of 'nipping round the blindside'. Rugby League provides our cultural adrenalin. It's a physical manifestation of our rules of life, comradeship, honest endeavour, and a staunch, often ponderous allegiance to fair play. *Colin Welland*

I don't fear no one but God. Another boxer might knock me down, but only God can make it permanent.

John Tate, US boxer

I want the fans to know that White Sox management will scheme, connive, steal, and do everything possible to win the Championship pennant . . . except pay increased salaries.

Bill Veeck

Moscow is in Russia, sure. But the Moscow Olympics won't be in Russia, if you follow me. *British Olympic committeeman*